# IN THE FIGHT

True Stories of Fighting for the American Worker

By Rich Michalski

Edited by J.A. Foley

ISBN: 979-8-218-69825-6 (hardcover)
ISBN: 979-8-218-69826-3 (paperback)

First Edition: May 2025

Cover design by Matt Scully

*For John Michalowski*

*Without you, I would not have
these stories to tell.*

# Table of Contents

*FORWARD* .................................................................... 1

*PREFACE* ................................................................... 3

*THE LOCAL* ............................................................... 9

    The GE Strike ......................................................... 10

    Committee Man ...................................................... 12

    The Shitshow – I Mean, "The Learning Experience" .......................... 14

    The Power of the Press ................................................. 19

    Kenny .................................................................. 21

    The Road to Politics .................................................... 26

    Carter Deregulates .................................................... 30

    Reagan and PATCO ................................................... 31

*THE BUSINESS REP* .................................................... 35

    Union Man ............................................................. 36

    Two Pairs of Pants .................................................... 37

    The Private Industry Council ......................................... 40

    Lunch with Jack ...................................................... 42

    Guide Dogs ........................................................... 45

    Representing .......................................................... 48

*THE LEGISLATIVE & POLITICAL DIRECTOR* ....................... 53

    The Striker Replacement Bill ........................................ 55

    NAFTA ................................................................. 56

    A Wolf Among Airlines ............................................... 63

    F-16s to South Korea ................................................. 65

    Jet *Bleu* ............................................................. 68

The 2-Ply Problem ............................................................... 69

The Fight for Bennie Thompson .................................. 71

Sparrows Point ..................................................................... 72

Walking for Cesar .............................................................. 76

Sitting Down for Leon ..................................................... 76

*A THOUSAND CUTS* ..................................................... 79

The Airline Pension Fight ............................................. 80

Standing Up to Rahm ...................................................... 84

Gunning for Progress ...................................................... 87

Becoming a Superdelegate ......................................... 90

The Tanker Deal .................................................................. 92

The Matador Cometh ....................................................... 98

Into the Trees with Weyerhauser ........................... 100

High on the Hog ................................................................. 121

*SPEAR IN THE HEART* ............................................... 127

Smoking Hot ......................................................................... 128

Progress in the Golden State .................................... 132

To Lose, France! ................................................................ 136

WTF, WTO? .............................................................................. 138

Daschle Threw the Snow .............................................. 140

*BATTLES WON, BATTLES LOST* ........................... 145

The Asbestos Fight .......................................................... 146

Lifting All Boats ................................................................. 152

I Was With Her ..................................................................... 154

The Train Leaves the Station .................................... 157

*FOCUSING ON THE FUTURE* ...................................................... *161*

    The 423 Building ............................................................... 162

    Building Schools with UPS ......................................... 163

    The Big Boy Scout Hat .................................................. 166

    Goats for the Old Goat ................................................. 168

*THE INTERNATIONAL* ........................................................... *173*

*AFTERWORD* ............................................................................ *191*

# FORWARD

My career has been filled with incredible experiences, beginning the moment I became a machinist. I've been witness to some pivotal moments in American history, as well as some hilarious ones. I love telling these stories, but they never would have been organized into a book without the encouragement of my wife, Nancy. On a special anniversary a few years back, she gave me a wonderful present, accompanied by this letter…

*Happy Anniversary!*

*Our courtship, wedding and 10-year marriage are the greatest romance made for movies. Travels around the world, once-in-a-lifetime events from Presidential Inaugurations to the Kentucky Derby and Packers Super Bowl, fabulous parties hosted, creative pursuits shared especially the design and remodel of our home all surrounded by music, laughter, joy, and a deep love for life and each other.*

*Your personal life, on the other hand, is the greatest novel. Full of exquisite details of the boy from Milwaukee a born leader who rises to the national stage in Washington DC and fights for workers. A man with clarity of purpose who enters every battle ready to fight and win for working families. Your experiences are a long string of extraordinary stories set on the national stage from the Oval Office to the Halls of Congress, Governors' offices, Fortune 50 Board Rooms to local Councilman Offices. The battles you have fought are of national importance and historic. You enjoy sharing these stories and we all love hearing them. They deserve to be shared in full glorious Rich Michalski detail on the page for posterity.*

*My gift to you for our 10<sup>th</sup> wedding anniversary is a book of your life stories written in collaboration with writer John Foley.*

*All my love,*
*Forever yours,*
*Nancy*

# PREFACE

Labor unions have improved the life of the American worker. This is not an opinion, it's a fact. Unions have been the driving engine for change in the workplace ever since our country broke away from England and started walking on its own two feet.

Higher wages.

Reasonable hours.

Decent health care.

Safety on the job.

Worker's compensation.

Unemployment and retirement benefits.

Unions built all these things at the bargaining table. Workers fought for each one of them with strikes and picket lines. At its core, capitalism values nothing more than the almighty dollar. Workers formed unions to remind die-hard capitalists that there are living, breathing people at the heart of these companies, and that there is nothing more valuable than *them.*

Major League Baseball is the perfect example. Even back in the 1970s, professional baseball players were making hundreds of thousands of dollars. There was nothing wrong with their salaries, to be sure – but there was no safety. Outfielders chasing a ball would crash into the back fences and sustain injuries. Then the union stepped in.

The Major League Baseball Association, the union that represented the players, made the demand at the bargaining table to put padding on the outfield fences. Hearing that, other stakeholders spoke up and agreed, and padding was added to the outfield fences. It took a union bargaining agreement to get safety in the baseball stadiums.

There has always been strong anti-union sentiment among business leaders. In general, they give unions a bad rap. Maybe some deserve it at times, but any instance of greed on a union's part is far outweighed by the benefits they provide. It not only gives the workers a feeling of unity and belonging and value, but it actively manifests a better quality of life for them. Then, whatever is driven by the bargaining table spills over into the non-union workforce. These improved working conditions become the rising tide that lifts all boats – companies afraid of being unionized offer workers this better quality of life up front.

The benefits are so profound, they resonate into the workers' lives outside of the job. It wasn't called "infrastructure" back in the 1950s and '60s, but unions and companies were constantly investing in their local communities, improving them with bridges, schools, parks, and any facility the area needed. That was a golden era of growth because everyone was making money, from the heads of companies down to all the workers. People could pay their taxes *and* buy new cars. Life was good. There was a healthy work/life balance.

That was the scene when I stepped into the field

I was 19 years old, and I accepted a job as a welder at GE. At the time, the very end of the '60s, the manufacturing industry was prospering in my home state of Wisconsin, as was farming and tourism. Big companies hired thousands, and small companies flourished as well, particularly those in value-added industries like manufacturing, which engaged a multitude of smaller contractors.

Our union, the IAM – the International Association of Machinists and Aerospace Workers – has always been a leader in fighting for labor law reforms. The "machinist" category is dynamic and multi-faceted because it encompasses all levels of labor from top-tier, high-performance, value-added work down to the simplest service and maintenance. Other unions supported change in the workforce too, but their interests were more narrowly focused.

Nevertheless, unions were a balm for the American worker. They gave workers an organized, collective voice that allowed them to stand up for their rights in meaningful and effective ways. Add to that a feeling of unity, of belonging to a group that shares your same concerns and interests, and you have created a more confident, more relaxed, and more productive worker. In the 1970s, almost every American industry enjoyed union representation, including manufacturing, service, technology, public, government, aerospace, retail, and warehouse.

When I joined GE X-ray, life was good for the American worker. Domestic industry was booming. The balance of power in the workplace was sane and sensible. The labor force in our country was expanding, and the fair wages and benefits that people were earning, thanks to the unions, helped usher in the golden age of the American middle class. Employees had pensions and good annual salaries. Suburbs were developed. Communities were formed.

But by the end of the 1970s, with Jimmy Carter standing against labor law reform and initiating major deregulations in the fields of energy, air transportation, and trucking, the undermining of the unions had begun.

By the end of the 80s, the presence of union representation in American industry would be diminished and the middle class would begin disappearing.

By the end of the 90s, union representation would be even less, and the middle class would be virtually gone.

The beginning of the end started with Jimmy Carter. He fell the first domino by shutting down a coal strike. Then he proceeded to institute several anti-union laws, all the better to please his big business constituents. Ronald Reagan picked up that baton and continued the momentum. George H.W. Bush kept it rolling, of course, and then in stepped Bill Clinton.

*Finally,* we all said to each other, *someone who will help us stop the bleeding and triage the middle class.*

But no.

Instead, Clinton hammered the final nail – the North American Free Trade Agreement.

With NAFTA in place, middle class jobs, especially manufacturing jobs, left the country. Give companies the option to pay lower wages, provide no benefits, and operate in deregulated areas, and how can they deny those substantial budgetary savings? Almost overnight, manufacturing disappeared from the American work force. GE, at one time the world's largest manufacturer, closed its plants, stopped making things, and moved into the financial sector. This caused communities built around local factories to find themselves without jobs, just in time for the dawning of a new millennium.

Over the next two decades, this generation got older and had children, but nothing improved financially. At this point, there was hardly anything left in their savings accounts. What's worse, the next generation would have no better luck finding jobs than their parents did. They certainly wouldn't be able to afford buying a home on their own.

The population that was once the American middle class grew disenchanted with their government. They were angry that their jobs went overseas and across the border. They felt burned, abandoned, betrayed.

In 2016, these masses became the base of Donald Trump's presidential campaign.

Trump gave them hope. He told them he was on their side. He planted ideas of broad conspiracy, stoking their anger toward other nationalities, promising to end the madness and make America great again. After two decades of hardship, the once middle class felt their almost-biblical sense of being forsaken shift to an almost-biblical sense of having found a savior.

Because they were so impassioned, because they were so desperate, and because there were so many of them, they succeeded in putting Donald Trump in the White House. Twice.

Those are the broad strokes. I'll use the rest of these pages to fill in the details, specifically about the legislation that undercut unions, the corporate greed that influenced politics, and the changing effect this all had on what was once the most contented, most industrious, and most well-paid generation of American workers.

I was there, in the fight, my team always proudly on the side of the workers and their families, amplifying their voices. Whether during my early role as president of the local, my time as business rep, my legislative director days in Washington, or even my years as General Vice President of Headquarters (GVP) of the union, I always championed the American worker. We fought for workers' rights, domestic jobs, and future prosperity. And we won a good many of those battles.

Sadly, we also witnessed some of the deepest gashes to the fabric of America, which contributed to the disillusionment and destruction of the middle class. American workers began to sour with resentment and grow heated with anger.

This book spans my 45-year career in the labor movement from 1970-2016, where my team and I had front-row seats to the federal mishandling of, not just unions, but the good people who built the second half of the twentieth century. I record these stories on the following pages in the hope that I move people into action. We need to vote in legislators who will reverse the detrimental policy decisions and greed-motivated actions that destroyed the American middle class. Without pro-union legislation, the American worker will continue to suffer and be exploited.

So, let's start at the beginning.

When I came into the field, the strength of the unions was at its peak, though none of us knew it at the time.

# THE LOCAL

It was the end of 1967, and I was 19 years old. General Electric hired me to weld X-ray machines, even though I didn't know how. It didn't matter because the company paid for my training. In those days, I was hungry. I wanted to make as much money as possible. Welding was demanding work, but I could take it. My father had been a machinist, so I felt it was in my blood. I was young, strong, energetic, and I worked fast. Also, landing a job at GE gave me a sense of pride – *this was the big league!* – but still I wanted more.

I found a second gig to fill my nights. I'd work the first shift at GE, welding the X-ray machines, then head over to the second job where I'd weld truck frames on the second shift.

Like I said, I was young and energetic. I kept that double shift schedule for three years.

Early on, I joined the union.

I found it empowering. I was part of a collective voice. My thoughts and feelings were amplified by like-minded colleagues. Instead of feeling like one of the millions, I felt like I had clout and leverage. Being part of that collective voice, my work had more meaning.

Of course, being part of that collective voice also means not shying away from doing what's best for everyone, even if it causes some personal inconveniences.

# The GE Strike

During this period, the VP of Human Relations at GE was a man named Lemuel Boulware. He reported directly to CEO Reginald Smith. Boulware had been with the company for twenty years already, and he was notorious for his hardcore negotiating tactic, which was not to negotiate at all. In any and every bargaining talk with the union, he would present a take-it-or-leave-it proposal, refusing to entertain any other ideas and intimidating the room with his seniority and iciness.

Big business saw unions at the time as a necessary evil. Unions hindered the process of outright capitalism by championing human rights. It was obvious to everyone that unions improved workers' lives, but to a company man like Boulware, who was tasked with keeping the workers' needs in check, unions were thorns in the company's paw. Of particular frustration to upper managements everywhere was the way one industry's union could inspire another industry's union to stand up for more. This was the case in our October 1969 talks with Boulware – we saw what was possible and took the leap.

The United Auto Workers union had made tremendous leaps and gains in the areas of pension and healthcare. Other unionized industries took notice and began fighting for the same benefits themselves. Big business owners saw this, and their panic quickly rose, as though raging wildfires were consuming their companies.

"The UAW is going crazy!"

"This is out of control!"

"It'll end us all!"

But while the UAW was getting its demands met, Ford was selling cars hand over fist. People were buying Mustangs faster than Ford could make them. The auto industry was positively booming. Automotive companies were making more money than ever, *and* workers were getting their fair share. We machinists saw that happening and knew it could happen at GE too.

We presented Boulware with our demands.

Predictably, he hardly dignified them and responded with his patented take-it-or-leave-it offer.

This time we were emboldened enough to leave it. It was my first strike.

I admit I was a little scared. When you go on strike, you don't know when you'll be returning to the job. An indefinite amount of time with no income panics everyone eventually. By the same token, I was in my young 20s and I was skilled, so I wasn't too deeply worried. If necessary, I could find work somewhere else. Plus, I still had that truck-welding second gig at night.

Something else that made the strike more bearable was how large and far-reaching it was. I certainly wasn't in it alone. Over 160,000 workers from GE plants around the country revolted, encompassing every sector of the company from appliances to locomotives to jet engines. It was a national strike, and it got national attention. Three and a half long months later, it was finally settled in New York through coordinated bargaining at the table.

When all was said and done, the strike had ended up securing all GE workers an extra three cents an hour. The bigger picture here, though, was the power of that strike. We taught GE a lesson, showing it that we were not afraid to stand together and fight.

I believe the strike taught us that same lesson.

We had felt the strength of our numbers, and it was a reassuring feeling.

# Committee Man

I was drawn to this idea of standing up for justice in the workplace. I saw unions as doing very good work, and I wanted to help. I ran for shop steward in 1970 and won the election. The steward's job was to communicate union news to coworkers and to guide them through union benefits and procedures as necessary.

I ran for reelection the following year and won again.

The same thing happened the year after that, and again the year after that. By 1974, I had been shop steward four years in a row.

The company announced to the people of Milwaukee that it was going to grow the medical arm of the business. In addition to X-ray machines, it was diving into the newest tech of the day, CT scanners. The company announced it intended to open a new facility in the Milwaukee area, which would provide thousands of jobs, but…they needed to shut down the workers' incentive plan to make it happen.

An incentive plan is a reward system for diligent work. In GE's case, it was that you'd build so many things, you'd receive a bonus. GE calculated that the model was not sustainable when stretched across such a large number of workers and so required the program's termination before proceeding.

I supported the bargaining committee's positions, and I was proud to do so. For the workers, the benefits of thousands more jobs for the community, and a more secure future for the younger generations, far outweighed the loss of the rewards program. The workers agreed to switch off the incentive plan. GE then made good on its word and opened an enormous facility twenty miles west of Milwaukee. The plant manufactured CT scanner equipment and went on to employ thousands. It felt good to be part of the process of helping the community, my community, strengthen and better itself.

I decided to run for a position on the bargaining committee. I was on the ballot for a plant-wide Tuesday election to be held at the union hall. On Monday, just the day before, I was on the ballot to be re-elected as a steward. When I lost the steward election, my manager Fred Ryker came up to me with a gleam of triumph in his eyes and said, "You've been such a pain in the ass, Michalski, and now that you're not steward, you won't last through the month!"

Sadly for Fred, I won the position on the bargaining committee the next day, with the most votes cast, in fact. Fred wasn't happy. He couldn't fire me after all.

This put me at the table with company management where I could help negotiate deals for the workers. By now I was in my mid-20s.

A few years later I stepped up to become chairman of the bargaining committee. This role opened me up to life outside of my ecosystem. I was second-shift committee man, which covered all five GE facilities in the greater Milwaukee area and required me to travel around to the five different locations. I really enjoyed that aspect, driving over to one place one day, another place the next.

Quickly thereafter, I became vice president of our local. A "local" is what we call the union branch of that specific region. It's also known as a lodge or shop. This was all happening so fast. The union work was starting to take up almost as much time as my GE work.

Then the president of our local left, and I filled the role.

All this transition happened in just a matter of years.

Throughout that entire time, I observed those above me, listened to those around me, and continued to widen my perspective.

At 30 years old, I represented 2,500 local lodge members.

I ran for president the following year and won. Then again the following year.

Then again, and again, and again, for a total of eight years. I liked being president. The job was to champion workers' rights to company leadership. I would take meetings with company brass when I had a concern, and they would take meetings with me when they had a concern. This dynamic suited me. I was a communicator, a peacemaker, a defender, a negotiator, a strategist, and a leader.

But my favorite part was the travel – those five locations were spread out over the entire Milwaukee area. I wanted to build trust, so I decided to meet the entire body of membership to get to know them and hear their concerns. As a result, I traveled to and fro around the area throughout my entire time as president, visiting these members here, talking to those members there, pressing the flesh, communicating whatever my message was at the time, hearing their issues, taking note, and moving on to the next location. There was a political aspect to the job, which prepared me for what would come next.

I grew into the role. It brought out my strengths and helped me hone them. Not everything ran so smoothly, however.

## The Shitshow – I Mean, "The Learning Experience"

When I first became president, I managed well, but there were a few areas where I was a little green. The most epic – and tragic – example of this happened on July 11, 1979, at the State Fair Park Coliseum, located right there in the center of Milwaukee. It was supposed to be a simple contract review and vote. It didn't go quite as planned.

We had just negotiated a new tentative contract, and it was a good deal. All the employees were familiar with the issues at stake, and the general consensus was that the negotiations were a success. All that remained was to make it official with a formal vote. We needed to get as many members as possible in one place, read them the contract in its entirety, note all the changes from the previous version, take any questions, and then conduct a vote.

The company agreed to allow employees out at noon on whatever day I scheduled the meeting. The State Fair Park Coliseum, I thought, would be the perfect venue for this. It could hold our number in its bleachers, and it had a fence all around it, containing the area. We'd be able to lock certain entrances and exits to control the crowd. We rented it out for 2 p.m. on a Wednesday.

This was the first time I was in control of all these logistical details. Next to the Coliseum is the Milwaukee Mile Speedway where they would run the Indianapolis races every Memorial Day weekend and the Miller 200 the next weekend. We got the infield of the speedway to use as parking. We got Muzak to set up the sound system. We brought in a stage for the middle of the arena, which was all dirt – it was usually used for horse and cattle shows. My team of ten and I would sit on the stage, and from there we'd be able to see all the members. It was going to be perfect.

The big day finally came. It was far from perfect.

My team and I got to the State Fairgrounds together, and as soon as we started pulling in, a policeman stopped my car. "Who's in charge of this event today?" he asked me. I told him I was, and I explained what we were doing.

"Okay, this is how this works," he told me, pointing to the Speedway. "You're going out there and getting your attendees to stop racing on the Speedway immediately, or I'm taking *you* to jail!"

I did not envision the day starting like this. We drove to the parking area and saw our members drag racing. We waved them over and put an end to it. That part was easy.

Then we walked over to the Coliseum, and I saw right away that something was very wrong – Stan, the head of the vote counters, was slumped over and asleep at the check-in table.

We had about 50 volunteers to help execute the event. Good, responsible people. Today, their baser instincts took over, however, and they decided to hit the bottle before coming to the meeting. Some folks got out of work early, and others didn't bother going in at all. But what they all did do was hit the bars. Then, when they got to the Speedway parking lot, they tailgated, cooked food, drank some more. I knew all this happened as soon as I put two and two together – the racing and now Stan's snoring. Stan is one of the best and most responsible of the volunteers!

"Oh, shit, look at Stan," I said to the team. "Shit! If Stan's been drinking, everybody's been drinking. This is not good."

And it wasn't. We damage controlled as much as we could, rounding up the volunteers. We brought a few back into shape and realized who was too far gone to help. As we did this, I saw members handing cases of beer to each other over the fence of the Coliseum. I also realized we were powerless to stop it because all our volunteers were drunk.

"Let's just try to start the meeting," I told my team, hoping it would bring some order to the chaos. We assembled on the stage, and as we got settled, a drunken gang of shop stewards came up and grabbed the microphones. They began ranting to the crowd about the contract, drunkenly getting the details all wrong. Luckily, we had given everybody "cheat sheets" with the changes to the contract outlined, and all the information was there in black and white.

"We're rejecting this deal! Strike! Strike!" they yelled.

I was momentarily stunned. Where the hell did this come from? We had vetted these changes through the members just days ago. It was a good deal with a terrific wage increase. These people were undoubtably out of their minds.

We turned off their mics and got them settled down with everyone else.

I started the meeting again. Finally, there were no more distractions, and I was able to begin reading the contract. I read it, plowing forward and going through all the clauses. It felt good. I had regained control.

Then the wind started up. I kept pushing through as the sky went from a calm, clear blue to rolling grey clouds. The wind got stronger. From above, the Coliseum was shaped like a big donut – the spectator seats were covered, but the middle of the stadium opened up to the sky. As the wind picked up speed, it began to feel like a tornado. All the papers on our table flew into the air, and the wind drowned out my voice in the microphone. Nobody could focus. The grey skies began to crack with lighting, rain got mixed in with the wind, and the icing on the cake was that all the power in the arena suddenly went out.

"Get the police here quick!" I yelled into the ear of one of my team members. There was a small police station on the premises of the State Fairgrounds, and a couple of my guys took off for it. I instructed the rest of the team to walk around and tell people to stay calm. We did that, and it partially worked. The police arrived, including my buddy from earlier who threatened to throw me in jail. They were not happy with me.

"Can I borrow a bullhorn from you guys?" I asked. They gave me one.

I tried to address the crowd through the howling wind and rain, but they couldn't all hear me at once. I decided to go from section to section, announcing. "Look, we're canceling the meeting! We'll reschedule for this weekend! We'll be in touch soon with the new time and place! Go home safely!" I repeated this from group to group. Some people were terrified by the sudden weather, and others were terrified at how drunk and wild their coworkers were acting. Near the end of my rounds, I came across a pretty bad group. These guys were totally wasted and acting like animals.

"Hey, guys, come on!" I said. "What are you doing?"

"Fuck you!" one of them yelled.

"We're voting for a strike!" another said.

Then something whizzed past my arm and hit the ground behind me. It was a beer can. Full. They hurled another one, and I ducked. I ran in a serpentine fashion away from them, and that's how my first big union meeting as president ended, with me dodging full cans of beer.

Later that day, when we had cleared everyone out of the State Fairgrounds and I was back at home, I made two phone calls.

The first was to the company. I had to let GE know we couldn't ratify the contract. That was a rough call to make. The guy on the other end of the line, a man named Jerry Winkler, went silent on me. "Jerry? You still there?" I asked.

"When?" he asked.

"You're gonna have to wait," I said. "But I'm trying for this weekend."

My second call was to the Milwaukee Chief of Police, a guy named Harold Breyer. I'd met him in the past and we had gotten along okay. I was hoping he could help me out.

"Harold," I said. "Listen, I've got a real fucking problem here."

"Yeah? What is it?" he asked.

I told him what happened. "And now I still need to schedule this meeting," I said. "I want to use a high school, but how do I go about that? Can you help me make it happen?"

"What high school do you want?"

"Just something where I can fit about 2,500 people. Don't some of those auditoriums or gyms hold 3,000?"

"Let me make some calls," he said. Then, on my behalf, the Milwaukee Chief of Police called the school superintendent and set it all up for me. He called me back and told me so.

"Great," I said. "Can I do it at eight in the morning on Sunday?"

"You got it. I'll even throw in a group of my guys to help you keep the peace. They'll be at your service."

Sunday rolled around. Everyone attended. Everyone was sober. We started at 8:00 and ended at 11:30. Everyone voted in favor of the contract.

And I learned big time from that entire experience.


# The Power of the Press

When I became president of the local, one of my first initiatives was to increase union membership. GE at its core was anti-union – all big companies were – and as such, it had a strict rule that it would remain an "open shop." This meant that workers were not automatically dues-paying members. It was a very divisive policy and completely unfair to the actual members who were paying dues and bettering the work environment to the benefit of all.

About 75-80% of the 2,500 workers were paying dues, which meant at least 500 were freeloading off the others. Not only did they skate by while enjoying the better pay and working conditions, but they also had automatic union help and representation if they ever got into trouble with the company. The National Labor Relations Board (NLRB) mandated that the union *had* to represent every employee, even if that employee did not consider themselves a union member.

So now, how could I convince the freeloaders to join up and start paying dues when there were no consequences if they didn't?

As President, I had my own committee, and I made it our first step to discern the freeloaders from the actual members. That wasn't difficult. Next step was to ask the freeloaders to sign up, explaining how it would be beneficial to the entire body of workers – their colleagues and brothers-in-arms. That tactic was mildly successful. We moved the needle a bit. But not enough. We needed a stronger strategy.

One thing I did as president was take over the union newspaper. I appointed a whole new staff and put the printing press, a Gestetner duplicator (if anyone remembers those!), in my basement. We published a paper every two weeks, reporting on what was happening in the company and in the medical equipment business. We'd bang out the article topics during my meetings with the bargaining committee, where we'd talk about what was happening in each department of the company. The tone of the paper was friendly, and it was all about the job. We'd spotlight different departments, advertise job openings, and provide pertinent information. Everybody read it.

While brainstorming strategies to recruit the freeloaders, it dawned on me that we could use the newspaper. I began to get vocal about the problem in our articles. If there was a threat to workers' rights, such as the dismantling of insurance benefits or unreasonable work rules, I would basically say that this was the fault of the freeloaders. I brought attention to the fact that we were not united. The company would not be taking advantage of us like this, I said in the articles, if we were unified. The freeloaders are affecting our quality of life, I would imply.

Then I started printing the coupons.

Once a month, the paper would have two coupons. NOMINATE THE FREELOADER OF THE MONTH, they read, providing a space for a name. The directions were to write the name of a freeloader you knew on both coupons, then give one to that freeloader and give the other to your shop steward. The shop stewards were the union representation in each department.

This plan worked like a charm.

Members on the shop floor wrote up the coupons like crazy. Some freeloaders would come back from their break to find fifteen on their desk from coworkers. The campaign was a success, and membership shot up fast. When we started, more than 500 workers were not paying dues. By the end of our efforts, that number was down to 5 or 6.

It made my job easier. Now everybody cared. We were unified. Secretly, GE was happy about it, though they would never admit it. With workers unified, a harmony set over the workplace and productivity ran smoother. The company also began to understand two things about me – I was both a reasonable man AND a great organizer of workers. I helped resolve disciplinary meetings, I helped implement new practices on the shop floor, and I addressed any employee issues that arose. When the Chairman and CEO of the company, Jack Welch, requested lunch with me, I knew I had begun to make a difference.

# Kenny

Before I was president, before I was even chairman of the bargaining committee, back when I was still a welder on the floor, a friend of mine, who happened to be a coworker, approached me with a request one day.

"Think you could make a backrest for my motorcycle?"

This was Kenny, a real good guy. Shy, conservative. Vietnam vet. "I'm riding to Sturgis, South Dakota," he said. "Gonna drive through the Badlands. Maybe even pop over to Yellowstone."

I was more than happy to help and welded together a nice, comfortable mount for him. We chrome-plated it and connected it to his motorcycle. Now he had a more comfortable ride, giving him something to lean against as he drove. Kenny was grateful. I told him it was my pleasure, and he took off on his summer trip.

He made it to Sturgis safe and sound and enjoyed a nice vacation.

It was his trip home that ended in tragedy.

Taking a northern route back, he cruised through Minnesota. As he coasted down a street with the right of way, a truck, not heeding a stop sign, hit him broadside. The truck dragged him a bit, then ran over him.

Fortunately, this happened literally blocks from the Mayo Clinic. Paramedics were on the scene quickly. They found his arms and legs crushed and his skull cracked. They took him to the hospital, lowered his body into ice to slow his metabolism, then began the long process of rehabilitation.

Quiet and shy as he was, Kenny was also a fighter. He survived. He had to remain in the hospital for a long time, of course, but eventually he was released. He moved back into his parents' home in a suburb of Green Bay. Because he was a vet, he had access to excellent rehab resources.

The first time I saw him after the accident, he was in a wheelchair and couldn't speak. One of his legs was now four inches shorter than the other, and he had steel in both to help rebuild bone. As physical therapy, he would walk the gravel road from his parent's farm to as far as he could stand it, then walk back. He did this over and over, year after year after year.

In our GE contract, there was a provision that essentially said if you took medical leave and did not return within a certain period, you'd lose your job. The technical explanation was that you'd "lose the right to gain seniority." Kenny's rehabilitation took him outside of those parameters, and the company let him go.

About five years after the accident, he called me up. He had brought his muscles back to workable strength. He had trained his brain and mouth to speak again. He felt ready to come back to work.

"Can I come back, Rich? I'm rehabilitated. I'm clear to work. Bring me back on, I'll do anything!"

By now, I *was* chairman of the bargaining committee. I had learned how to give and take at the table. The company had let Kenny go due to policy and precedent, but my view was that this was an exceptional situation. Having nothing to do with the fact that Kenny was a friend, I felt this precedent needed to be challenged. The man had been in a serious accident, and he miraculously survived! His body was compromised, sure, but his mind was as sharp as ever and he *could* handle some of the work we had at the company.

First, I went around to Kenny's old supervisors and appealed to them. No dice. They flat-out refused to rehire Kenny. A big part of that was because there was no way he could lug around heavy materials, which encompassed a lot of what we did there. I couldn't argue with that. But another aspect, which was plain to see, was that department management just didn't want to deal with Kenny's limited abilities. They were being lazy. They were being prejudiced. They were being unfair.

This got my fire roaring.

Kenny couldn't manage heavy equipment, but tech was rapidly evolving and getting more sophisticated. The company assembled X-ray machines, and now the new thing was CT scanners. The need was growing for specialized, delicate, clean work using highly advanced and, more importantly here, *lightweight* materials. Why not bring him back on and train him in a new position, one he could handle? Who could argue with that?

GE could argue with that. They hid behind the technicality that he had been on leave over the allotted limit per company policy. My position was that the company policy was open to interpretation. I suggested we create a new precedent here. I was determined to get him rehired. Kenny was a good, decent man. He needed to make a living, and he was willing to do any work that was asked of him. I saw the bias in the system with crystal clarity, and I vowed to fight it. Not just for Kenny, but for all the Kennys out there and in the future. I was operating from a "union" state- of-mind. I was putting the rights and the wellbeing of the workers first.

My moment came on a Friday night after regular work hours, when I was called to a late meeting at the detector facility.

The detector facility was where we made detector arrays for CT scanners. This was in the early days of the machine. The heart of a CT scanner is this "detector array," a sophisticated assembly of parts that serves to translate the X-ray readings into images. There were three of us at this meeting – the manager of the facility, me, and Sam Koutas, General Electric VP of Human Relations.

Sam was a New Jersey man. Big, tall, and Greek. Always with a cigar clamped between his teeth. Once a Navy submarine commander, now he was a reserve officer. We got along well, Sam and me. We had a way of hashing out any issues between the company and the employees with satisfactory resolutions for all.

The issue on this night had to do with a large number of the detector facility staff. The work there required employees to be specially trained and to meet a certain standard of quality in their work. Many were not meeting that standard. Our meeting's goal was to coordinate the transfer of a number of employees to different departments. I realized then that if the facility needed new workers, I had a prime candidate.

"Listen, Sam," I said, "this work is perfect for Kenny. Let's bring him back and train him on CT detectors assembly. He can work right here!"

"Not happening," Sam said, shutting me down. "Next issue…" And he went on discussing employees that needed to be transferred. I watched, listened, and sometimes contributed as Sam and the facility manager solidified the plan. Finally, they both felt good about it and turned to me. They needed my help to execute it all.

"Sound good, Rich?" Sam asked. "You'll do it?"

"Yeah," I said. "I'll go along with all these things. No problem. But you have to do something for me."

"What's that?"

"We're bringing Kenny back on. He'll work here in this department."

"Fuck you!"

"No," I replied. "It doesn't go that way. It's fuck *you!*"

Sam blustered. "You're out of line! That is NOT happening! I told you to forget it! I can't believe you're pulling this shit!" He stormed out of the meeting.

The facility manager and I looked at each other. We made small talk for a few minutes. Then Sam came storming back.

"Okay, we'll do it. He can come back to work. Now will you do your part?"

"Of course."

And Sam kept his word. After all the refusing, all the arguing, all the justifying, GE rehired Kenny and put him to work in the detector facility.

Six months later, GE featured an article on Kenny in their employee newspaper, a high-quality periodical it disbursed on a national level to all employees. Photos of Kenny ran alongside text praising the company for its humanity, its nobility, its benevolence in bringing a disabled ex-worker back to work in a new position he could handle.

I rolled my eyes, but the irony and hypocrisy of it all didn't bother me one bit. I got the man back to work. The union had gotten the man back to work. Kenny went on to spend another twenty years at GE, and he is happily retired now.

# The Road to Politics

I suppose it's a natural progression to move from leadership positions into politics, but that's not where I expected things to lead. Nevertheless, the next decade of my career would see me expanding my leadership abilities and traveling more, which in turn prepared me for the following decade of my career, where I found myself pushing legislation and actively working with labor- friendly candidates and representatives.

My first brush with politics was long before all that, however. It was 1979. The next presidential election was approaching, and the union was supporting Ted Kennedy. As President of the local, I answered to the director of the district, a guy named George Lajsic. Kennedy was coming to the UW campus in Steven's Point, Wisconsin to kick off his campaign in the state, and George was going to be part of his entourage, showing that the union backed him. George directed me to be there too, for more union visibility and to help spread the word.

I was to travel to Steven's Point with a guy named Joe Spirit. Joe had a big van with a new paint job that read VOTE FOR KENNEDY and four giant megaphones on the roof through which he played "Happy Days Are Here Again." We were given a bunch of Kennedy buttons to sell at the rally as well. Joe and I were fine with this assignment. It was something different and it would probably be fun. The only problem was that Steven's Point was a two-hour drive for us, so we had to leave early.

Joe and I hit the road at 5am. We pulled into the Steven's Point area around 7:30. A few miles from the rally location, we passed a local bar that not only looked open for business but had a packed parking lot. A heavy smoker, Joe turned to me and said in his raspy voice, "We should stop for a beer. We got time."

"Joe, it's 7:30," I said.

He nodded. "We should stop for a beer," he replied, pulling into the parking lot.

We entered the bar and learned that it was the day of the Pacelli High School's Homecoming game. As a yearly tradition, the bar opens early and gives free drinks to the alumni as a sort of pregame party. The crowd was drinking, and they were in a great mood. Joe and I looked at each other, smiled, and I went out to the van to get the buttons.

We sold every one of them. The bar patrons were overjoyed to have us join their party, and we had a terrific time. We toasted Kennedy. We toasted the local high school. We toasted the alums. We toasted the bar. Meanwhile, my boss George was in the car with Ted Kennedy, heading to the college, and they passed the bar. I can only imagine how George's eyes bugged out of his head as he saw Joe's unmistakable van with VOTE FOR KENNEDY painted on its side parked right there in the lot. This was before cell phones, and even before pagers, so he couldn't contact us. They rolled right by, continuing on to UW. His anger just had to simmer inside until we showed up, which we eventually did. Once he got us out of earshot from Kennedy, he swore up and down and gave us hell.

But he was happy we had sold all the buttons.

That incident didn't stop George from keeping me involved in Kennedy's campaign. The following spring, the candidate was coming to Serb Hall in Milwaukee. "You're going to introduce him," George told me.

Serb Hall, a place we commonly used for union gatherings, has a capacity of about 2,000. I'd addressed crowds there before, but this seemed like a bigger deal. This was politics on the national stage, and I was expected to come up with some one-liners and a short speech. I was more than a little nervous. I still had not personally met Ted Kennedy, nor anyone of that stature. It was a new league for me.

That's one of the reasons I embraced it. As nervous as I was, I wanted to do it.

The night of the rally, I was prepared but still anxious. The actor Robert Foxworth was also there. He could tell how I was feeling, and he tried to calm me down. "You'll be okay," he told me. "You're gonna do fine. So, you're introducing Kennedy. But guess what – I'm introducing you!"

And he did. He said a few words to the audience, then introduced me. Hearing this Hollywood celeb saying my name and calling me out to the stage felt good. It legitimized my own role introducing the candidate, at least in my mind. It helped steel my nerves.

After he introduced me, I got up there, said my piece, and introduced Kennedy. Then Kennedy, full of energy, barreled out onto the stage and did his thing.

I had no way of knowing at the time that my involvement in his campaign was only just beginning.

Shortly after the rally at Serb Hall, Wisconsin voted in the primary, and Kennedy won. That entitled him now to have delegates. "I want you to run to be elected as the delegate," George told me. "We're in the fourth congressional district of Wisconsin. Kennedy only gets one delegate here, and I want that to be you. Can you get that done?"

I told him I could try.

Five or six of us ran for the position. The favorite was a guy from the UAW who seemed to have all his ducks in a row. The vote was to happen on a Saturday at 12:30 in the afternoon at a local community center. Each candidate would stand up in front of the crowd and make their stump speech, then all those in attendance would vote.

*Okay,* I figured. *This is a numbers game.* It would come down to how many supporters I had in the voting caucus. I had never done anything like this before, so I had no structure to rely on here. I was still president, so I had my committee and my core group. They would be there for me, but it wasn't enough. I heard the UAW guy not only had tons of supporters, but he was also catering a lunch at the event to gain more popularity.

My chances did not look good.

The fact was that I did know enough residents in the district to secure a majority vote, but the guys I knew would never show up on an early Saturday afternoon for something like this. In fact, I remembered, most of them played in a softball league every Saturday morning, after which they'd all hit the bars, get shitfaced, then go home. The vote was going to occur at precisely the same time they'd each be on their second or third beer. How could I persuade them to forego such a treasured weekly tradition for a very sober, and arguably boring, voting event at the community center? All they'd find there would be speeches, not a drink in sight, and maybe my opponent's free food.

*My opponent's free food!*

I made the call to my friends. "Look," I said, "You gotta do this for me. You have to come to this thing and vote for me. After the game, come to the community center. I'll tell you what – there's gonna be free food! Come and eat lunch, vote for me, then you can go on your merry way. Please."

It worked. The day arrived, and almost the entire softball league showed up. I filled the room. My friends got in line for the UAW guy's

29

free food, enjoyed a good meal, then made their way to all the front half of the seats in the auditorium. One by one, the candidates took the stage and introduced themselves. When I got up there, my guys started cheering. "Woo, Rich! We're voting for Rich! Yay, Rich!" I didn't have much to say. I didn't know what to say. But that didn't matter.

I won by a majority vote. The UAW guy was pissed.

And I stepped into the world of politics.

# Carter Deregulates

Throughout this stage of my career, Carter was in the White House and, unfortunately, he was launching an anti-union executive order. He was a democrat, but he was trying to appeal to the right and big business. The first thing he did in office was kill a national coal strike that had been going on for over 90 days. There were 160,000 people on strike. Carter killed it by executive order, completely undermining the power of unions.

Then he deregulated oil and gas. We tried to fight it but to no avail. In the winter of 1978, the president of IAM wanted to stage a demonstration at the Hilton on Michigan Avenue in Chicago where oil and gas executives were gathering to rally for some deregulation legislation. I organized my people to protest against it, putting together a team of eleven. That was the good news. The bad news was that, for some reason, we didn't have enough cars. We all had to pile into one. It was terrible – there were about eleven of us in a Ford station wagon. I drove.

Miraculously, we got to Michigan Ave safely and began marching outside the hotel. The windows were open, and the gas and oil execs were standing there in the windows giving us the finger. It was a very hostile vibe. And despite our efforts, the deregulation went forward.

Not long after, Carter deregulated air transportation.

Then he deregulated trucking. There were five basic trucking companies at the time, all organized by the teamsters. Truckers got benefits, living wages, healthcare, and pensions, among other benefits. To please big business, Carter allowed companies to start using independent contractors if they wanted, which they certainly did because it allowed them to save money by not offering benefits. They paid the contractors in cold hard cash, and that was the end of it.

This was a thumb in the eye to all the good work unions had been doing since the 1940s. Companies had been growing and adding jobs. Union membership had been growing. There was successful investment in infrastructure. Carter pulled the thread that began the unravelling of all of this. His deregulation opened the door to the corporate raiders of the 1980s, the Frank Lorenzos, the Carl Icaans, the Steve Wolfs.

This was also the reason for Carter's defeat in the 1980 election. He was a democrat, but he was catering to republican values. Unions and other liberal organizations backed real democrats, like Ted Kennedy, in the election. And republicans, when faced with a wannabe republican vs. a real republican, will go for the genuine article every time. That's how Ronald Reagan got into office.

# Reagan and PATCO

In the 1980s, big business could not have been happier. What Carter started, Reagan continued and took further. In the first year of his presidency, he dealt a blow to the American labor movement that would change everything moving forward.

The Professional Air Traffic Controllers Organization (PATCO) went on strike in August 1981. They were protesting unfair wages and long work hours. They had no reason to expect Reagan to work against them. He had promised many times during his campaigning that he would take care of the PATCO members and look out for them. In fact, PATCO was the only labor union that was pro-Reagan. They supported him.

He did not return the favor.

On Day 1 of the strike, he made a speech from the Rose Garden demanding in no uncertain terms that all 13,000 air traffic controllers on strike either return to work in the next 48 hours or face termination. Then he twisted the knife. He recruited people who would cross the picket line – military controllers, air traffic students, retirees, and more.

Unfortunately for the labor movement, his plan worked. Replacement air traffic controllers reported for duty right there on the first day. It wasn't enough to cover all the strikers, but 50% of that day's scheduled flights flew. The following day, with clear, blue summer skies and no troublesome storms, 75% of the scheduled flights flew. Thirteen thousand air traffic controllers had gone on strike, but the world continued the same as ever. They could not make their point because Reagan compromised all their power.

The president's intimidation tactic persuaded some of the strikers to return to work, but the union did its best to stay strong. When the 48-hour deadline passed, more than 11,000 PATCO members were still standing together…and they were all fired.

A couple months later, Reagan decertified PATCO.

The bubble had burst, and the narrative began to change. Big business realized that with the government's backing, it did not have to kowtow to unions anymore. It realized it could be tougher with unions and with workers. Along with that, people began viewing strikers not with sympathy and understanding, but with disdain. Strikers were no longer seen as people uniting for fairness, but as ungrateful and selfish lawbreakers.

The next year, Wharton published and widely disseminated a manual that encouraged business leaders to learn from the PATCO strike, and business leaders did learn. From that point on, strikebreaking was common. Copper miners in Arizona went on strike, and they were all fired. Paper workers in Maine went on strike, and they were all fired. Meat packers, bus drivers, and more experienced this same thing. Meanwhile, businesses were actually forcing these strikes so that they could fire the union members and bring in scabs.

Unions were still around, but now they operated with a lot more caution and a lot fewer strikes. A decade later, Clinton would make matters even worse with his Striker Replacement Bill, but at the moment we were all just stunned by Reagan's actions, and the snowball effect they'd had. We realized that if we were to stand up for the American worker, we'd have to fight in careful, smarter ways.

# IN THE FIGHT

# THE BUSINESS REP

As president, I was still on the GE payroll, and I still technically had duties within the company, but more than anything I was an agent of the union. The way I saw it, most of the job was to create and maintain harmony between the workers and their bosses. My secret strategy for this?

Listening.

At heart, I'm a people person, and that's exactly what the position required. Previously, union matters were settled by one side strong-arming the other into submission. My tack was to do my best to become a partner to whomever needed my help, to make them feel heard. I did this on both sides, with the union members and with the company brass.

It was an effective strategy, though it called for me to talk to everybody all the time. I took a humanistic approach, which was welcomed and appreciated. But this was more than just corporate diplomacy. I was getting things done. Instead of barking out orders, though, I collaborated. I created new job classifications, which created new jobs. I increased our productivity and raised our quality.

The powers that be at the Machinists Union noticed my work,

and after eight years as president of the local, the union asked me to come work for them full-time. It was now 1985. The new position, a business rep for the union, would require me to represent workers much in the same way I had been representing my GE coworkers, but the scale would be exponentially increased to multiple companies across Wisconsin. I'd be involved in day-to-day problem solving and contract negotiations. I wouldn't be working for GE any longer. I'd be a full-on union man through and through, working directly for IAM. I said yes.

# Union Man

While I was leaving GE, I wasn't really leaving GE because it was one of the companies on my docket. The new position had me representing a third of the district, specifically:

- GE Medical (2,500 members)
- GE Hotpoint (12 members)
- GE Service (25 members)
- Eaton / Cutler-Hammer (600 members)
- Mercury Marine (1,800 members)
- Alumatic (75 members)
- Kelvinator (200 members)
- Ladish (800 members)
- Deltrol (250 members)

They were all in Wisconsin, but not all in Milwaukee. The job required me to travel around to them constantly, and that was fine by me. As I mentioned, I liked traveling. I liked the adventure. More than that, I loved to *learn.* I soon realized that every one of these companies was its own animal, and each one had something to teach me.

A good example is the company Ladish. This is the company that built the Trans-Alaska Pipeline. It's a huge facility, and it's the home of the "seamless ring." The way they forge it is by taking a 25,000-pound steel cube and heating it until its molten. Then they take a ram with 850,000 tons of power and pop a hole right through it like a donut. Then they roll the cube, constantly hitting it with fire, until it's a perfect circle. The result is steel pipe about twelve feet high, twelve feet deep, and two inches thick all around. These would then be used for various industrial needs such as pipelines and aerospace programs.

The CEO of Ladish was a man named Vic Brown, and he was a legend in the business world. At 96-years-old, he was still running the company and playing golf. I requested a meeting with him and asked him, in front of the entire committee, what the secret of his success was. He answered without missing a beat: "I always look for a better way to do something than I did it the day before."

There was no hesitation with his words, and there didn't seem to be any forethought. They were right there already on the tip of his tongue. And it was such a simple, core philosophy. Never be satisfied. Always improve. What I did yesterday is yesterday's business, but today is a new day and maybe I can do it better.

Vic's wisdom stayed with me for the rest of my career.

# Two Pairs of Pants

I was on the job for maybe a month when GE reached back out to me to invite me to go to Japan with my old bargaining committee. The purpose of the trip was to visit different manufacturing facilities like

Mitsubishi Electric and Hewlett Packard and observe any advanced techniques for manufacturing that could help GE.

At the time, Japanese companies were embracing the philosophy of W. Edwards Deming, a business theorist and management consultant who introduced the concept of "quality circles" to Japan after WWII. In a typical factory, line managers held about 85% of the responsibility for quality control, whereas production workers only held about 15%. Deming thought that was wrong and needed to be reversed. He believed production processes should be redesigned to more fully account for quality control, and all employees should be continually educated on quality control. American businesses did not go for this theory, but the Japanese embraced it.

The union agreed it would be a good idea for me to accompany my old team at GE on this trip. In fact, I was to be the spokesman for the group, along with a counterpart from GE – the head of manufacturing for medical systems. This was going to be a big deal, and to make sure we didn't screw anything up, the company had us spend over a week with a professor at the University of Wisconsin in Milwaukee. Every day, he would spend a couple of hours with us, teaching us about Japanese culture. GE wanted us to be comfortable, but it also wanted us to be careful. The goal was for us to be good representatives of the American people.

The lessons were fascinating, especially the etiquette lessons. One thing I learned was how to handle a business card when you're handed one by a Japanese businessman. What you do *not* do is put that card right in your pocket. No, you hold it out and study it, and read everything on it, because the person who gave that to you is watching you. It's almost as though you are holding them themselves in your hand. One wrong move could sour the whole relationship.

With new cultural knowledge under our belt, we were ready for the trip. We flew to Japan. Knowing the Japanese affection for golf, we brought along golf clubs as gifts.

One day, after taking a tour of the Hewlett Packard plant, an executive took us to a break room to get some rest and have some refreshments. We were all wearing the blue shop coats HP made their employees wear. The executive lit a cigarette, I grabbed a cup of coffee, and I started making small talk with him. We went back and forth asking each other questions. Every time I'd ask him a question, he'd answer it and then immediately ask, "What about you?"

"So, do you like to travel during your vacations?"

"Oh, *hai,* yes! I love to travel! What about you?"

"Yes, I love traveling too. I love meeting new people. Have you ever been to Europe?"

"*Hai! Hai!* I've been to Europe – to Italy and France. What about you? And this went on for a little bit. Everyone in the break room was casually listening to us talk. Eventually, I asked, "Do you play golf?"

"*Hai!* I like to golf, yes. What about you?"

"Well," I said, "I do, but not on days that are too warm because I like to wear two pairs of pants…in case I get a hole in one."

He looked blankly back at me. The whole room fell silent. He turned to someone from his team and began speaking in Japanese. Others joined them.

"Oh, you fucking did it this time," my counterpart from GE quietly uttered to me. "I think you pissed him off. Good fucking job."

"Fuck you," I uttered back.

Suddenly, the Hewlett Packard team erupted in laughter. They had gotten my joke. The exec came around the table, patted me on the back, then gave me a big hug. Everyone relaxed, and it was the perfect ice breaker to the afternoon.

I was tempted to pull that joke out a few more times over the trip but decided to spare my team the groans.

# The Private Industry Council

One of Reagan's private sector initiatives was the Private Industry Council. This was a local committee set up to discuss and make decisions about businesses in the area. It was created for and comprised of business leaders. Labor union reps were welcome to join, but they could not be chairperson – that position was always for business leaders only.

The county executive appointed me to the local council, and I sat on the board. It was good for me because I got to know all the business leaders at the table over time. I spoke up for the workers when I saw the need, and as a result, I wasn't their favorite person, but they did learn that I was reasonable.

The main purpose of the council was to mainstream people from welfare to work, training them and helping them to earn a living. The training was done mostly by churches and private training facilities. A subcommittee of the Private Industry Council, the selection committee, decided which facilities would get the government funding for training. While labor reps could not become chairman of the Private Industry Council, they could be appointed to chairman of the selection committee.

I was appointed.

This position was a big deal. It managed tens of millions of dollars every year, doling it out to the training programs. The deal was that however much the training program received, they could keep 25% of it for administration. In other words, if we awarded a place $100,000, whoever owned it kept up to $25,000. I wanted to do the job right, so I had my committee vet all the training facilities and churches. I also had them report on the trainees' performances and statuses.

We found so many abuses, it was staggering. Most of these

abuses were found in the church programs. We learned that hardly anyone was proceeding from these trainings into the workforce. Instead, trainees were simply being moved from one training to another, and then to another. These corrupt organizations were playing musical chairs with people!

We began doing surprise visits at these places and cutting back on awards. Visiting one Baptist minister, we found a beautiful Mercedes-Benz with gold wheels parked outside his church. We decided to stop funding that one.

The minister did not like that. He showed up at our next meeting with his lawyer and some other people.

We asked the police to attend as well, just in case it got out of hand.

I'll never forget sitting at that table with my stalwart vice-chair and a kindly, soft-spoken man who would take over the selection committee when I left. We sat across from the minister, a hulking guy wearing gold chains, gold rings, and diamonds. Next to him was his wife and his lawyer.

"Can we just get enough funding to train 25 people?" the lawyer was asking.

"No, we're closing this one down."

"How about 20? Can we do 20?"

"No, the program doesn't work, we're shutting it down."

The minister suddenly jumped out of his seat and smashed the table with both fists.

It startled us. The table bounced from the impact, and I was sure the soft-spoken gentleman next to me was going to have a heart attack. It was a crazy scene for a moment. Mercifully, it ended without incident.

As unnerving as that scene was – and there were plenty more like it – I took pride in doing what I could to stop corruption and fix the labor gaps in our community.

# Lunch with Jack

Jack Welch was CEO of GE from 1981 to 2001, and during those 20 years he was the CEO that all other CEOs admired and copied. He not only grew the company and took it into new areas, but he singlehandedly changed how big business viewed capitalism. Before Jack stepped in, GE was already very conservative, very anti-union, but it was following a common model that included investing in people with programs like pension plans and investing in new products. Jack took a different approach.

He quickly earned the nickname "Neutron Jack," because he laid off over 100,000 people in his first years as CEO. Like a neutron bomb blast, the buildings are still standing, but the people are all gone. Jack believed a smaller headcount and lower labor costs would lead to higher profits. More than that, his primary philosophy was that the stockholder was God.

Previously, GE had a long-term outlook where they would take the profits from every quarter and disperse some of those funds to research and development, to develop new products. For 100 years, ever since Thomas Edison and J.P. Morgan founded the company, GE was focused on building electrical products – medical equipment, jet engines, light bulbs, household appliances, and much more. Jack changed that as well.

He saw the money for R&D as low-hanging fruit, and he took it off the table to put it in the pockets of stockholders as dividends. It was paramount to him that the company provide stockholders dividends every quarter. To fulfill this, he cracked down on quotas. If any department came up short from their projected earnings, he'd punish the management. To find more profits for dividends, he began selling off product lines, anything GE wasn't first or second in.

What's worse is that now business leaders around the country started looking at what Jack was doing and thinking, "This is a pretty good idea. I'm going to do that with my company." And they did.

Welch's dedication to stockholders, and those CEOs that adopted his same practices, built the Wall Street of the 1980s, which inspired Oliver Stone to make the Wall Street movie with its most famous line delivered by Michael Douglas: "Greed is good." The federal government had no problem with Jack's system overhaul, as Ronald Regan was fully on board with big business (plus he had been a GE spokesman on the GE Radio & TV Hour for ten years).

As companies jumped into this much more cut-throat form of capitalism, they squeezed as much money as they could from local managements and from any employee benefits. Soon, they started owing money to their own pension plan programs, and now their pension plans were liabilities. The solution was just to get rid of them, which many did, unless they had a union protecting them. And if they did have a union protecting them, that's when company brass would try to force strikes, try to get the union members out of there so they could simply hire new un-unionized people.

In the second half of his career, Jack implemented a policy called "stack ranking," which the employees began calling "rank and yank." It was a process where managers would rank their staff, assigning them to one of three categories. The top performing 20% were considered rank A. The middle performing 70% were considered rank B. The final 10% were considered the sub-par performers, rank C, and they were fired. This became an annual process. No matter how well the company was doing, tens of thousands of employees would be laid off every year. It created a nervousness among the workers and put team members in competition with each other.

Then, later, as soon as NAFTA was passed, Jack took full advantage of it and shipped thousands of jobs overseas.

Many future CEOs were groomed at GE as proteges of Jack. They went on to continue Jack's practices as they led such companies as 3M, Home Depot, Albertson's, Chrysler, and Boeing. Stack ranking is still a practice today in companies like Microsoft, WeWork, and Uber. Jack's legacy of toxic work environments and short-term profit goals continues to exist.

I first met Jack before he was CEO. He was still a VP, and I was 29 years old. We met for lunch because I was president of the local at the time, and it was a simple meet-and-greet.

The second time I met Jack, he *was* CEO, and I was a business rep. I got the call that he was coming into town and wanted to meet with me for a private lunch. The location would be the GE campus in Waukesha. We'd meet in the office of VP John Trani (who would later become the CEO of Stanley Works), but Trani would not be part of the lunch.

Learning this, Trani called me up.

"Rich! You're having lunch with Jack? What are you going to talk about, what are you going to tell him?" He sounded nervous. Trani and I had held some tough meetings about one of his initiatives, which he called "Focus 80," and which I re-termed "Fuck us 80." It was all about cutting costs and outsourcing work.

"That's none of your business, John."

"Yes, it fucking is! You gotta tell me what you're gonna tell him!"

"I'm not telling you shit."

"You can not have a meeting with him without telling me what's going on!"

"I'm not telling you anything."

The truth was that I was not going to speak ill of him, but it was fun playing with him on the phone like that.

The facility where we met was very grandiose, like a palace.

There were huge, plush offices lined around the perimeter of the building, where managers of different product lines were based. But the center of the building was almost like a separate entity, it felt like a house within a house.

I gave my name to the receptionist, and she cleared me to step into the inner sanctum, complete with skylights and fancy furniture. Then I had to present myself to a second receptionist, who cleared me to continue into the belly of the beast, where the nicest offices were, and meals were prepared by a private chef. That's where I met Jack.

Turned out that Jack had no agenda, no ulterior motive. He just wanted to meet for a get-together. He began the lunch by thanking me for all my help and cooperation. This was during the time when Jack was gutting a lot of GE's branches and sending workers to lower-paying outside contractors. I replied that my goal was to ensure the stability of the remaining workforce. "Jack, I hope you're going to keep your word that you'll keep a viable workforce here in Milwaukee. These are good people. They've been loyal to the union, but they've also been loyal to the company."

He said, "Look at the numbers, Rich. Look at what I'm doing to the other locations and not to yours. I have not done that to your people, and I won't."

It hit me that I had won Jack Welch's respect. This was a big deal, and it served me well for the rest of my career, particularly when I became the legislative & political director.

# Guide Dogs

In 1948, a 57-year-old member of the Machinists Union went blind. His family tried to get him a guide dog, but their request was denied. Guide dogs, they were told, only take care of young people. This man was too old. When the union found out about that, members grew enraged. The only way he could get a guide dog was to buy one, which cost about $50,000. So, the local people raised the money and bought him a guide dog. Thus was born Guide Dogs of America, non-profit organization founded by the Machinists Union and still active today.

Getting a guide dog is a big process. It requires you to go live for a period at the Guide Dogs of America school in Sylmar, California to learn how to work with the dog. There is a big area on the campus that is like a backlot, where they set up houses, roads, curbs, and other city aspects. They continually change the environment so the blind students learning to work with the dogs can get used to being in the real world.

The dogs go through quite a process as well. First, the potential guide dog would be put in a foster home for a year so it can get used to living with people. After the year, they move the dog to Sylmar where they X-ray it for hip dysplasia and bone disease, two disqualifying conditions. Then they neuter or spay the dog and do whatever final preparations are needed to prep the dog for the person.

When one of our members was in attendance at the school, the director, a man named Bud Melvin, used it as an opportunity to appeal to me. He called me up and shared the school's financial woes with me, telling me how much they had to spend on veterinarians and the X-ray procedure.

"Do you think that GE could get us an X-ray machine?" he asked.

At first, it sounded like a very over-complicated and unmanageable ask.

But then I thought, *why not?*

I called the VP of Medical Systems at GE. "I need an X-ray machine."

"What? What are you talking about, Rich?"

"An X-ray machine."

"What the hell do you need an X-ray machine for?"

I told him the story, and added, "Look, we can make this into a great PR thing for GE. Let's get some guys to donate their time and rebuild an X-ray machine from parts for the school. Then we can publish stories saying, 'See what our workers did!'"

It didn't take long for GE to get on board. The optics were good – a beneficial partnership of GE, the IAM, and the guide dog school in Sylmar.

Then the school called me again. "Rich, we need to set up our vets with a good operating room, a surgery room, where we can do the X-rays and perform procedures on the dogs. You think GE could help us with that too?"

I called GE back. "You know what, now we need a room for the X-ray machine."

"Oh my–Jesus Christ, Rich!" After just a little back and forth, he agreed: "Okay, tell them it's a yes."

GE spent a lot of money that day, and it was good for everyone. We had a big presentation ceremony for the new room and new machine. I flew out to California. There were movie stars and soap opera stars at the event, then we all went to dinner on the Queen Mary in the Churchill Room. When it came time to order the wine, everyone turned to me.

"Rich, you order the wine!"

Here I was, the head of a table with California bigwigs, union leaders, and corporate leaders. And together we had just done something so very good for the world. I felt good, really good. But at heart, I was still just a local guy from Wisconsin.

"Uh, I don't know anything about wine," I demurred. "Why don't you pick it out?"

All in all, it was a first-class night.

# Representing

Of course, as a business rep, most of my hours on the job were dedicated to representing workers who needed union help. Sometimes they were being treated unfairly by the company. Then again, sometimes they were in the wrong. Whatever the case, whether they were guilty or innocent, my job was to defend them in a way that ensured they were treated fairly. That doesn't mean we lied for them. If an employee stole from the company, they were going to be fired and that was fair. We were there to make sure they were treated like human beings.

Say a guy gets kicked out of the house, and he's sleeping in his car. Now he's down and out and not thinking straight. He does some stupid things, maybe drinks before going into work. He screws up on the job, and everything goes wrong for him. What do you do with a guy like that?

If you're the union, you help the guy out.

His manager might say, "I don't like that guy, I'm going to fire him."

I'd say, "No, you're not going to fire him. He deserves a break. Let's work with this."

That's what the union is for.

The NLRB in Milwaukee knew me well because I represented so many different shops. One time, they called me to fight for a guy named Tony, who was the president of a local lodge. I already knew Tony, and he was a difficult guy. He had a mean streak, and he was abusive to his managers, calling them names and denigrating them up and down. In fact, I had just seen Tony two weeks ago in one of our meetings. He was very bullheaded in the meeting, demanding that his company was being unfair, when in truth they were meeting all our demands.

"Tony, what is wrong with you?" I asked. "Don't you see they're giving us everything we want?"

"I don't care, this is wrong!" he shouted, and he remained antagonistic through the whole meeting. He was also on workers' comp at the time for a bad back.

The head of relations from Tony's company gave me a ring. "Rich, can you come in tomorrow?"

"Why?"

"We got Tony on video."

"What do you mean 'on video?' What does that mean?"

"You know he's out for workers' comp with a bad back?"

"Yeah."

"Well, we got him on tape working another job installing air conditioners."

I went in with Tony. On the other side of the table was the relations manager and his staff. They showed the video. Tony had no explanation. He was fired.

That was a bad day for Tony.

A few days later I got a call from the NLRB. They started to talk about Tony's situation, and I cut them off. I told them I already knew all about it.

"Well, what are you going to do about it, Rich? You have to arbitrate this."

"I don't have to arbitrate that!" I told them. "I only arbitrate situations where the company does something wrong. In this case, the guy's on video, using his back! He supposed to be out for a bad back! This isn't a losing battle, he's already lost!"

Here's another situation that was pretty cut and dry. A worker was leaving the factory after his shift one snowy evening, walking rather stiffly. Security guards outside the plant took notice of him when he slipped on some ice just outside the gate and went down hard. They watched as he struggled to get up with no success. They went over to help.

What did they find?

The man could hardly move because he had wrapped a 50- foot copper cable, a welding cable, around his body, weighing him down with an extra 150 pounds. He was trying to smuggle it out.

It didn't go well for that guy.

Then there was Reginald. He worked in the polishing and plating department, where they would use high-carbon steel saws to cut strong steel. Sometimes those saws would break, at which point they'd be thrown away.

Walking out of work one day, Reginald was caught by security with a large knife, almost like a machete. "Hey, this was obviously a saw blade," they said to him. "What happened? Did it break, and you polished it up? That's illegal, you know. It's company property, and you've turned it into a weapon." The company had a hard line on stealing. It meant automatic discharge.

Reginald quickly replied, "No, this is my brother's knife. I just brought it into work to buff it up and sharpen it."

Now, Reginald was a very nice guy, and nobody really wanted to see him fired, so they called me in. My contact at the company was a guy named Al. He had jet-black hair, wore pants that were tapered down by his shoes, and he smoked like it was a source of oxygen.

"I gotta save this guy, Michalski. They don't want to fire him," Al said.

"Well, company policy is pretty clear," I said. The knife sat before us on the table. "If he stole it, that's it."

"I know! I know!" he groaned.

"You *could* say that you believe him and that he just had this knife."

"That's bullshit, though."

"Well, it's your bullshit. It's not my bullshit."

He just looked at me, and I could tell I got him thinking. He went to go confer with company leadership while I went to talk to Reginald and his local union rep.

"I think we're going to pull this off," I said. "I think they're going to buy the idea that the knife is your brother's. But here's the thing – don't let them keep it. You should ask for it back because it's yours."

A little while later, we were all in the disciplinary meeting, and the mood was light. They were not going to fire him. They gave him an official reprimand and a day's suspension, but that was it. Everyone was happy on both sides.

As we were wrapping up, I uttered to Reginald, "Don't you have anything to say?"

He met my eye, then looked over to Al and asked, "Can I have my brother's knife back now?"

The way Al suddenly glared at me made us all bust up laughing.

"Michalski!" he raged. "Michalski! Let's step outside!"

Outside, he blustered at me. "You motherfucker! You! How could you...you...why did you..."

I laughed. "Let him keep the knife."

"You motherfucker!" He was so upset, but he understood.

Later, I said to Reginald in private, "Look, we can all tell that's an old saw blade and not your brother's knife. But you're a nice guy and you're not being fired. In the future, don't push it."

Representing good people was always an honor, and I stayed in the business rep position for a little over five years. My experience, both as president of the local and as a business rep, had me dealing with all kinds of people and all kinds of situations. I learned the art of negotiations and how to work with different personalities to get things done. It primed me for the next stage of my career, which would become the longest stage – Washington, D.C.

# THE LEGISLATIVE & POLITICAL DIRECTOR

One key element to all the positions I held was building relationships with people.

After about five years as a business rep, I moved up to become the legislative & political director of IAM. All the relationships I'd built up to that point, and I had a lot of them, showed IAM leadership that I had cultivated a sphere of influence. They thought I could put it to good use in the halls of Washington, and I welcomed the new challenge. There were two overarching facets to the job – managing the political action committee (the PAC) and lobbying in Washington. It was 1991, and I was 42 years old. This was the beginning of an adventure that would take up the next 15 years of my life.

A PAC can raise as much money as it wants, so long as it comes from individuals. The union treasury is forbidden to contribute any money, so the job required a lot of fundraising. That was fine. It was easy to do and allowed me to interact with the communities, which I always enjoyed so much. We usually raised about five million dollars a year, though we could only donate a max of $5,000 to any given election. We could give a candidate $5,000 for their campaign in the primary election, and if they made it on to the general election, we could give them another $5,000.

This grew frustrating in that the number never increased. It was a frozen number. It was $5,000 forty years ago, and it's still $5,000 today. Meanwhile, the max amount of money *individuals* can contribute has been indexed for inflation every odd year and has grown exponentially. Unions are one of the biggest fundraising entities in the private and public sectors for candidates, and the government knows that. Unions represent the middle class of America, the working class, and Congress knows that too. By freezing the contribution amount at $5,000, the working class was being handicapped in the elections, virtually silenced, while super- wealthy private individuals were free to donate a lot more. In my new position, it was easy to see that dark money was moving around in the shadows of the political stage.

I realized that while our money might not get too far, other spheres of influence potentially could. Specifically, my specialty – people. Our members would be movers and shakers, knocking on doors, getting folks to donate to our candidates, educating people on the issues, mobilizing membership to do work for the candidates, and making sure people showed up to vote.

I worked with our members to decide which candidate we would back. We were thoroughly organized, which made all the difference. We had an agenda, and we measured candidates against our goals: community support, worker education, healthcare, and other holistic topics. Our agenda also helped us identify those candidates that we'd oppose.

Aside from managing the PAC and supporting candidates, the job required me to lobby legislation. I would collaborate with companies and then lobby for certain things. Boeing presented me an airplane trophy with the words BEST SALESMAN on it after I pushed the purchase of Boeing Airplanes by Midwest Express. I could make things happen.

We had to be our own advocates. There was never a time when we were 100% fully on board with everything a politician was doing. For instance, at the same time I was fighting Bill Clinton on NAFTA and PNTR for China, I was also pushing his Welfare to Work initiative with United Airlines. In fact, we successfully got a repair and maintenance facility built in Indiana where mechanics moved from high-rent cities to a location they could afford to buy a house. Like I said, we had an agenda. As we witnessed the slow, painful gutting of the American middle class, our agenda was to save it.

# The Striker Replacement Bill

The first thing the American Federation of Labor (AFL) did when Clinton got into office was introduce the Striker Replacement Bill to Congress, which was a Democratic majority at the time. The bill's purpose was to stop companies from the what-was- becoming-common practice of permanently replacing strikers. Reagan encouraged companies to do it when he was in office, and by now, in the early 90's, big business was not fearing strikes. Get rid of the troublemakers! Hire someone new who's not part of a union! This was not an illegal act, but we wanted to make it one. The bill would protect strikers and penalize companies that brought in scabs.

Previously, it had always been a gray area that nobody really understood. The National Labor Relations Act in 1935 pronounced it illegal for a company to fire a striker, but three years later the Supreme Court ruled that a striker could be permanently replaced. We wanted to clear all that up once and for all with the Striker Replacement Bill to ensure that a strike still served a purpose. Reagan had taken all the teeth out of it, and we wanted to put them back in.

Clinton himself agreed to sign the bill, which was terrific. The House then approved the bill, which was even more terrific. Now all we needed was sixty votes in the Senate for cloture. There were sixty sitting Democratic senators, so we were sure we had the sixty votes.

We did not get the sixty votes.

Two Democratic senators voted against it, both from Arkansas. Clinton's own senators.

And the bill died.

That told me, and it told all of us in Labor, that this administration probably would not be as friendly as we had expected.

# NAFTA

As one of his last presidential acts, George H. W. Bush negotiated the framework of the North American Free Trade Agreement (NAFTA), building in that it had fast-track authority, which meant Congress would have to vote up or down on it with no amendments allowed. They would not be able to change anything in the treaty; they could only pass it or reject it. It was a trilateral trade bloc among the U.S., Canada, and Mexico that basically allowed the three countries to use each other's resources for industry, agriculture, goods, and services. These resources included foreign labor. In other words, Mexico, which did not have such rigorous environmental, health, and safety protections, would directly compete with American blue-collar workers and American family- owned farms and businesses. To a company owner who only cares about the bottom line, Mexico's lack of regulations and labor laws was like Shangri-La.

On the campaign trail, Clinton promised to sign NAFTA. Once

elected, he picked up right where Bush had left off. He was pushing and plugging the treaty, trying to get the American public's buy-in. Mostly, he was pandering to the Business Roundtable, which happened to be headed by Jack Welch. Jack and his cohorts were chomping at the bit to get NAFTA implemented. Hilary Clinton's healthcare legislation was in the works at the time, so Jack made a proposition to the president: help us pass NAFTA, and we'll help you pass the first lady's healthcare. Clinton liked that idea.

He put Rahm Emanuel in charge of leading the fight. Emanuel had been Clinton's Director of Political Affairs, but he only lasted in the position for five months. He was such a brash man, with such a gruff personality, that he alienated people more often than not. After firing him from the political director role, Clinton kept him on as Senior Advisor for the next five years. As a task of redemption, Clinton charged Emanuel with leading the NAFTA campaign through Congress. Specifically, he had to appeal to the Democrats that were against NAFTA and turn their "nay" votes to "yea."

Most of the Democrats in Congress were against the agreement, and so were the unions. To say it was slanted in the favor of big business is an understatement. It allowed U.S. corporations to open plants across the border and use locally sourced labor. There was no requirement to pay unemployment, pay workers' comp, or offer any benefits. Wages were super low. It took jobs away from U.S. workers. All of this was already happening and had been happening since Reagan implemented free trade zones, but NAFTA would take this model and supersize it.

The worst abuses could be seen down in Mexico in the maquilas which had cropped up during the Reagan era. These were domestic corporate properties set up and being run on foreign soil. It was painfully obvious to us that we would have to fight NAFTA like we'd never fought anything before. If it passed, it would devastate communities across the United States. To prep for the fight, I went down to Mexico several times to check out a few maquilas just across the San Diego border. A professor from the UC Berkeley came along, as did a few others, and together we investigated these free trade zones from a human rights perspective.

Sometimes, armed guards kept us from getting access to a property, but we could observe terrible conditions even from the outside. Our typical day was to cross the border at 6 a.m. and get to the maquilas around 8 a.m. We would visit the people, who were always so humble and kind, and we would tour as much of the property as we could. We'd bring our own food to eat for lunch.

One day, we were having lunch in a community center built at the maquila. It was made of brick, but they had used many different kinds of bricks. Building materials for maquilas were mostly collected from factory scrap, so it was a hodgepodge of colors and styles. While we sat and ate in this community center, we looked out the windows, gazing at the hills of garbage all around this maquila. Gradually, we realized that things were moving in those hills of garbage. It wasn't a scrapyard – it was a sort of shantytown, a mess of cardboard boxes and pallets, with people living in them! Some had televisions with cables running here and there to provide bootlegged electricity.

How did it get to this point? Well, when the Mexican Revolution ended in 1915, land was taken from the plantation owners and dispersed to the people. Then, in the 1980s, the Mexican government amended laws to allow it to sell that rural land to corporations and the super wealthy, displacing the residents and forcing them to move to urban areas. Then the U.S. and other foreign corporations came in, bought the land, set up their plants, and hired local workers. With no federal safety mandates or regulations, the companies could make their own rules. This encouraged an environment designed to exploit the very most it could get from the workers. The maquila was born. With nothing to prevent terrible working conditions, maquilas were soon filled with all sorts of undesirable elements – drugs, prostitution, exploitation.

The Korean-owned companies had their version of these free trade zones too, and their maquilas were like miniature imperialist countries. Pregnancy was forbidden, and employees were compelled to get vaccinations that would prevent conception. If any unfortunate worker *did* get pregnant, management would force them to have an abortion.

This was all going on pre-NAFTA, and it wasn't about to get any better. What NAFTA would do is take down the fences around these maquilas and apply the whole model to a larger scale. It would be an untamed, uncontained version of trade with the sole purpose of exploiting the worker.

This was going to be a tough fight, but we had to try.

Later, back in the States, while Rahm Emanuel continued Clinton's campaign to persuade everyone that NAFTA was a good idea, I was meeting with my team at the AFL to figure out how to prove to people that it was a lousy idea.

There were about a hundred of us in the room. We were talking about the terrible conditions of the maquilas and how NAFTA would make it all infinitely worse. We talked about the prevalence of child labor we had observed, with kids as young as 12 working full shifts. The maquilas squeezed everything they could get out of every worker, and child laborers usually burned out by the time they turned 21.

"Look," I said to the group, "let's tell Bill Clinton that if he thinks this is such a great idea, he should send his daughter to Mexico so *she* can work at one of these maquilas for six months. If she gets home and says, 'It's all good, Daddy!' then we will support the agreement!"

"Hey, what the fuck?!" someone shouted.

"You can't say that!" someone else said. "You can't bring his *daughter* into this!"

"And why not?" I countered. "He's bringing *your* daughter into this! He's bringing your grandchildren into this! He's bringing their futures into this."

But it was an uphill battle to prove my point. Even organized labor was not unified against NAFTA. The teachers, the firefighters, the police, anyone who served the public just didn't seem concerned about it. "What does this have to do with us?" they wondered. "Why should we care what happens with NAFTA?"

"Excuse me," I said to them, "but you do know that our U.S. factories, the people in our U.S. factories, they all pay taxes, right? Well, guess where those taxes go? Infrastructure, from which you make your living! NAFTA affects you and your lifestyle because it directly relates to the tax revenue that pays your wages!"

But still, we could not convince enough people. Corporate greed was driving this campaign, and everyone who mattered was under its spell.

On November 17, the treaty was being voted on in the House of Representatives. I was with George Kourpias, the IAM president at the time, and we were waiting on the results of the vote with Washington State Representative Jim McDermott in his office. With Boeing being the largest exporter of value-added products in the U.S., Jim was 100% on board with NAFTA.

Clinton and Emanuel's strategy was to force the Democrats to vote for NAFTA even if they did not need their votes. In the beginning, anti-NAFTA democrats had a 50-vote majority. But the Clinton White House put never-before-seen pressure on all these Congress members to support the legislation, adding seductive promises to fulfill whatever needs they had in their districts. Minds were changed and, sure enough, NAFTA passed by more than 50 votes. A swing of more than 100 votes forced Democrats to turn their backs on core constituencies.

Reporters and photographers were also at Jim's office that day, and I landed on the front page of *USA Today.* "Supporters feel good about winning today…" the article began.

Well, Jim felt good. George and I, not so much.

A few days later, the treaty went through the Senate, where it was also approved. NAFTA was ratified, and it was as destructive as we had feared. For one thing, it paved the way for PNTR (permanent normal trade relations) with China, which opened the door for China to enter the World Trade Organization (WTO). Now our workers had to compete with the Chinese as well.

For another thing, it drove away the Democrats' working-class base. This was a direct assault on the working-class families, particularly in the Northeast and Midwest, but not exclusively. It was so devastating to people, yet so lucrative for companies that even those companies operating out of the Southern U.S. to avoid unions, they too were powerless to resist the lure of NAFTA- sanctioned Mexico. And with all the jobs leaving, the working class became disenfranchised. In both Nebraska and Indiana, blue seats flipped to red and stayed that way forevermore. This all contributed to the Democrats losing the House in 1994.

Bill and Hilary wanted people to believe it was gun control that defeated the Democrat majority, but it was NAFTA. The working class, both union and non-union, recognized that this reckless behavior by the government was putting their futures in jeopardy. They responded with their votes.

The leadership of the Democrat majority provided a room in the Capitol called the Doorkeepers Office as a safe haven for union reps. It was a place to congregate and collaborate. One day, in the middle of the NAFTA debate, I walked out of the Doorkeepers Office and bumped into Congressman Bill Richardson, Democrat from New Mexico, and he said to me, "We are going to win NAFTA, and we are going to kick you out of the Doorkeepers Office when this is all over." I could tell this was not an empty threat. As union reps, we were given credentials to enter the Capitol and congressional office buildings, but everyone could feel that the wind was changing.

Then, in January 1995, Newt Gingrich came into power as Speaker of the House, and the first thing he did was strip the credentials of union reps and close the Doorkeepers Office to us.

The next time I saw Bill Richardson, I stopped him on the street and congratulated him on fulfilling his promise.

NAFTA was a bust from the get-go, and we knew it would be. You can have a GM plant in Mexico today with 5,000 employees, but it would only need a parking lot for 50 because most of the workers won't be able to afford cars. I knew we were going to lose this fight, but like I said, it didn't stop me from trying.

Clinton's betrayal of working-class America did meet with a little poetic justice, though it doesn't give me much comfort. Remember the agreement he made with Jack Welch – once he helped Jack get NAFTA through, then Jack would help him get Hilary's healthcare through. Well, after NAFTA passed, Jack called a special meeting of his Business Roundtable in D.C., and they came out against Hilary's plan. Once the Roundtable got what it wanted, it promptly turned its back on Democrats.

During the NAFTA debate, representatives of big business flooded the Democratic Congressional Campaign Committee (DCCC) meetings, pushing the legislation. There were so many, that it became standing room only. After NAFTA passed, you could fit all the businesspeople that showed up at the DCCC meetings in a phone booth. They were gone.

# A Wolf Among Airlines

Carter's deregulation of airlines paved the way for corporate raiders like Frank Lorenzo and Stephen Wolf to come in, squeeze as much money out of the airline as possible, then leap out with a golden parachute as the company crashes into the mountains. To men like this, the almighty dollar was king, and the goal was to make as much money as possible without giving a thought to who might get hurt in the process.

Lorenzo was with Continental, where he finagled a leveraged buyout of the airline Braniff then moved on to Eastern airlines. At Eastern, he demanded sacrifices from his employees, and he made cuts. Then he asked for more sacrifices and made more cuts. In the meantime, he created a shell corporation as a holding company for all corporate assets and property. At the time, Eastern had more planes in their fleet than any other airline. They were a significant competitor in the aviation industry.

He then had the holding company charge the mother company rent for the airplanes it was housing. Then he added a penny on every gallon of fuel. Soon, the company was bleeding to death as it had to continually flow money into the shell corporation. He paid himself out well, screwed the Eastern employees, and left the company a wreck.

When Wolf became CEO of United in the early 90s, he continued his career of killing jobs by purchasing planes from France-based Airbus instead of Washington-based Boeing. Airbus wanted access to the U.S. domestic market, so they offered Wolf a deal. They'd provide a hundred planes for no money up front. He would only have to make payments on them when he started to use them. Wolf readily agreed. It was a windfall for the company to get this free access to capital without having to raise any. It was an unbelievable, unprecedented deal.

He also went after employee pensions. The way he ran the company took such an antagonistic stance towards the workers that he was afraid to fly on his own airline. Whenever he did, he brought his own food and drink, even his own drink glass. He wouldn't let the flight attendants give him anything because he knew how badly he had fucked them over, time and again.

Wolf left United in '94 and went on to US Air. I was dealing with a lot of legislative issues with United at the time, and an executive called to ask me to come out to Chicago. "Can you come out and see what Steve left behind?" So, I flew to Chicago, and we went down to the NBC building, where Wolf had signed a 20-year lease for the two top floors, the 29th and 30th. One of the floors was all business and administrative stuff. The man was six- foot six, and when I stepped up to the lectern he kept in the boardroom, it felt like it was set up for a giant.

The top floor, the penthouse, was where he lived. It was a huge, sprawling, plush apartment. He had a full kitchen, a full bar, and the shower was gigantic – you could fit 6 people in there easy. "We wanted you to see all this," my United contact said, "so you could see what was really going on here." They wanted me to see was that he was spending money on himself to excess while telling his employees they had to make more sacrifices. They wanted me to witness this so I could report to elected officials that United wasn't in bad shape due to the employees – it was *this* fucking guy.

Then Wolf went to US Air and did the same thing, including buying Airbus planes. Boeing's greatest competitor got exactly what they wanted, thanks to Steve Wolf. The deal with United cracked open the door for Airbus, then the deal with US Air blew it wide open. Wolf had helped the French economy, the French workers, the French companies, while at the same time stealing away jobs and opportunities from the American working class. Northwest followed in Wolf's footsteps and bought from Airbus as well, as did Delta.

Perhaps that's why Wolf would so often fly his own 737 airplane to a private landing strip he had in France, adjacent to a large, beautiful chateau. To this day, no one can prove he accepted the property as a bribe from Airbus. One can only speculate.

# F-16s to South Korea

I represented thousands of workers at General Dynamics in the Dallas-Fort Worth area. One of the products they built was the F- 16 Fighting Falcon, an offensive and defensive military jet. It was a light jet, fast and agile. In 1991, the company announced that it was going to sell 120 F-16s to South Korea. The deal had been approved by Congress, and local Democrat Congressman Pete Geren was helping the company usher it through. The governor of Texas at the time was also a Democrat – Ann Richards, who had just stepped into office. This was terrific news, and everybody was excited. This deal was providing a massive load of work to General Dynamics, which would help sustain jobs and possibly even create new ones.

Soon after, there was another announcement. A thousand South Koreans would be coming to Dallas-Fort Worth so that the IAM and some General Dynamics engineers could teach them how to build the F-16s. Then the South Koreans would go home and assemble the fleet themselves. So, there wouldn't be any new jobs created by this deal after all. Additionally, we would be transferring U.S. military technology to a foreign country.

This was no good. We had to try to stop it.

I contacted Ann Richards' chief of staff and asked her if we could get Ann's help on this. Our local union leader in Dallas-Fort Worth was very active in politics and had been very supportive in getting Richards elected. He was also appointed to several leadership committees to help the Democratic administration in Texas.

"Of course! The governor will definitely help!" she said.

So, we held a meeting and made a plan. We would host an afternoon public forum in the parking lot outside the plant and have politicians make speeches saying that they support the Texas workers. They would talk about how this deal would affect the entire community and ask General Dynamics leadership to amend it so that Texas could build the planes instead. Everyone liked this plan. Ann Richards was at the meeting, and she promised to do her part.

Later, I got a phone call from Pete Geren. He was raging. "Who the fuck do you think you are, holding a rally in front of the plant? In my town!"

I said, "What the fuck is wrong with you? These are *your* constituents! They're your people! It's not me – it's them! They want to do this, and we're going to support them."

We had been hoping Geren would see the light, but evidently that wasn't going to happen. At least we had the governor on our side.

Only we didn't.

The day before the event, her chief of staff called me.

"The governor won't be participating in the event."

"What? She won't? She's still coming, isn't she?"

"No, she's not."

This was ridiculous. The rally was not an anti-company thing. It was not an anti-trade thing. It was simply pro-jobs and pro- American. Obviously, Geren had gotten to her.

The local union leader immediately resigned from all his positions that aided Ann Richards. He told her, "I want nothing to do with you. If you can't stand with us, we're not standing with you at all."

We held the rally anyway, and it was staggering to see the amount of people that showed up. There were at least 25,000.

And we prevailed. The plan was scrapped. The sale was still going to happen, but the jets would be built by American workers in America. It was a great rebuff to the company's attempt at saving a buck by having the Koreans do the work.

There's a post-script to this story. As Ann Richards started looking at securing a second term, she reached out to IAM president at the time Goerge Kourpias for support. He said, "Look, Ann, if you can't settle things locally with your own people, we can't settle anything with you. You have to take care of the local people."

A little while later, Richards' chief of staff contacted me saying, "Ann wants to speak with you." She wanted a meeting with the union leadership. This was July '92, as the Democratic Convention was getting closer. The next gubernatorial election would be in 1994, and she knew that the machinists and other organized labor were cold toward her.

We met at the Hilton Hotel, up in the governor's penthouse suite. There were four of us from the union – George, the General VP Tom Buffenbarger, the Southern Territory GVP Ed House, and me. We sat down in her living room. Ann looked at us and said, "I think my chief of staff has something to say."

What was this? We all turned to the meek-faced chief of staff, and she said, "Um, I didn't communicate properly with the governor about that rally, and she wasn't aware that she was supposed to attend. The fact that she was not there is my fault."

We were stunned. Of course, we didn't buy that for a minute. She couldn't even admit when she was wrong, and she had to blame it on her chief of staff.

George W. Bush beat her in the next election.

# Jet *Bleu*

Another early 90s aerospace event was the certification of Jet Blue Airways. It was a new airline starting up out of New York City. They needed a certificate, and the request was to have it expedited. The company promised to buy Boeing planes, so my office got involved and lobbied the Department of Transportation and the FAA. We attended meetings with the directors and heads of departments in these agencies, and we shepherded the process along to the point where Jet Blue was aiming to buy more than a hundred Boeing planes.

Meanwhile, Airbus began sniffing around this deal.

Jet Blue got their certificate on a Friday. The company was going to announce its deal with Boeing on the following Tuesday.

Sunday afternoon, a Boeing V.P. called me and said, "We got a problem." Now that Jet Blue had its certificate of flight, they had canceled the news conference where they were going to announce the deal with Boeing on Tuesday and instead set up a joint news conference with Airbus on Thursday!

Just like with United Airlines, Airbus offered Jet Blue to take delivery of the planes for free. The entire fleet they would need would be parked in the Arizona desert, and the airline only had to pay when they wanted to roll a plane out and use it. Airbus had successfully found its way into the American aerospace industry.

Jet Blue ordered over a hundred planes with Airbus and put in a reservation for more in the future. All that talk about buying Boeing planes was a ruse to use us to help expedite the flight certificate. Jet Blue was going to be getting their planes from Toulouse, France, not the United States.

Throughout my career, I've done a lot of work with the aerospace industry. It didn't take long for me to realize that Airbus was always the villain lurking in the background throughout all these deals. Sometimes they won, and sometimes we won.

# The 2-Ply Problem

The IAM represented about 1,200 workers at Beloit Paper, a company based in Beloit, Wisconsin with a research center a few miles away in Rockford, Illinois. It had begun as a family-owned business but was purchased in 1986 by a heavy equipment manufacturer called Harnischfeger. Harnischfeger built industrial mining equipment – giant bulldozers, huge steam shovels, enormous drills. The manufacturing machines themselves were so big that the company had to build them first, then construct the facility around them.

Beloit Paper had been around since 1858, and the company was the lead contender in its industry, which is why Harnischfeger bought it. Beloit Paper was the premiere company on the planet for building the machines that make toilet paper.

Moreover, it owned the intellectual property of the machines which made 90% of all the toilet paper in the world.

As Legislative & Political Director, I had Beloit Paper in my jurisdiction. I quickly learned that the CEO was somewhat reckless. While actively heading the company, he physically detached himself from it by setting up his own office in an all-glass building on Lake Michigan in Milwaukee, where he could look out at beautiful vistas on the lake. He also bought a couple of jets, which he flew all over the place. He liked to spend money.

Unsurprisingly, in the mid to late 90s, about ten years after it bought Beloit Paper, the Harnischfeger Corporation went from a $40 stock to three cents on the dollar. It filed for bankruptcy, then decided to recoup come losses by selling off Beloit Paper's assets, namely the equipment, the intellectual property, and a unique giant lathe the company had developed (for use in building driveshafts for battleships and aircraft carriers).

A Swedish corporation put in a bid just for the intellectual property, and the sale was imminent. This would mean that the company would close and 2,000 people would lose their jobs. Quickly, I set up meetings with people in both offices – the Beloit one and the Rockford one. We selected several representatives from the community, our lawyers put together some papers for us calling out that this was a matter of national security, and we planned a trip to Washington, D.C.

We met with Clinton's team, and everyone in my group spoke, explaining how the closing of the business would impact their lives and the lives of those in their community. Then I explained that selling this intellectual property would stop Beloit from building the machines that made toilet paper, while at the same time it would not guarantee that the Swedish company would begin building them. What if the Swedes just sat on the intellectual property for whatever reason and never went into production? "When was the last time," I asked the board seriously, "that you could do without toilet paper?"

They laughed. They thought I was being cute. And they approved the IP sale.

All those Beloit workers, both union and non-union, lost their jobs.

And, sadly, this is just one story out of a hundred more just like it. The American middle class was not just being gutted. Now it was disappearing.

# The Fight for Bennie Thompson

In 1992, Clinton appointed Congressman Mike Espy to be Secretary of Agriculture, forcing him to vacate his Mississippi congressional seat, which was then opened for a special election. Several people campaigned for it, and the union backed Bennie Thompson, who at the time was mayor of Bolton, Mississippi. IAM was not alone in their support. All organized labor supported Bennie, including the UAW and the United Food and Commercial Workers (UFCW). As the mayor of a small town, Bennie was known to put people ahead of money.

The biggest businesses in the area were catfish farms, which were commonly called "plantations" because they covered acres and acres of land. The right-wing candidate who was running against Bennie colluded with the catfish farm owners to instruct their employees, who happened to be minorities, to report to work on election day and work all the overtime they were offered. This was an obvious attempt at voter suppression. We had some meetings and decided to contribute our political funds to rent trucks, vans, and busses to get people to the polls.

When the day arrived, we brought in vehicles from neighboring states in a coordinated effort to give those Mississippi residents a chance to vote. They had the right to vote, and we were not going to let them be denied. So, throughout the day, people loaded onto the busses and were driven to the polls. The right-wing candidate got word of this, and suddenly people in khaki uniforms showed up at the polls holding cameras. They began taking videos of everybody in the voting line, the implication being, *you're screwed when your boss sees this!*

The people we had in place there went immediately to the Justice Department. The FBI showed up at the polls and shut down the voter intimidation. This was during Clinton's presidency, and I do not trust we would have found the Justice Department as responsive if Reagan or one of the Bushes had been in the White House instead.

Bennie got elected that day and today – 29 years later – he is still an active part of the congressional leadership in Congress.

# Sparrows Point

There's a little area on the outskirts of Baltimore called Sparrows Point, where there is a shipyard once owned by Bethlehem Steel. The company decided to sell the shipyard in 1996, and I was asked to help oversee the details and take care of the workers who would be coming in with the new owner. The potential was terrific. We saw that we could put 2,000 people to work who didn't have jobs. What they would be doing is ship *breaking.* That's where they literally break ships, turning them into scrap and selling them overseas. I'd be working with the staff of Dutch Ruppersberger, who was the Baltimore County Executive at the time.

Bethlehem Steel had used corrosive chemicals and pollutants in that location over a period of years, and it made the sale of the shipyard tricky. The EPA has a rule – if your property has been found to be a Superfund site, meaning you've poisoned the ground, then it's your responsibility to clean it. And this was a Superfund site. Bethlehem Steel was a huge facility. Walking through, you'd see dead birds lying by dark puddles of water. Whoever bought the site was going to inherit the cleaning, and that notion scared off investors.

One investor who had shown interest was the then-owner of the Baltimore Orioles, Peter Angelos, a lawyer who had made millions on asbestos, coal mining, and cigarettes. Nevertheless, he was a good person. He was generous with the community. I began talking to him once or twice a week on the phone. Throughout a year of negotiations, we never met in person. He too, despite his money, was having misgivings about the cleanup obligations.

My team and I appealed to the EPA to break tradition in this case. We talked to them, we shared with them our projected numbers of how many people would be put to work after this sale, and we got a waiver for this particular case only. The EPA ruled that the entity that owns Bethlehem Steel would be responsible for the cleanup, even after they sell the property.

It was not an easy road to get to that decision, and I had to apply intense pressure to get there. After it was official, I called the White House and spoke to the woman in charge of the EPA and thanked her.

"Well, Rich, we've enjoyed working with you on this," she said. "We really did."

"You know, I hope I wasn't too pushy," I said.

"Please, Rich," she responded. "You were not pushy. You know who's pushy? Jack Welch is pushy!"

At the time, Jack Welch was on the hook for the Hudson River, and he had launched a PR campaign claiming that the contaminating PCBs "do not pose adverse health effects." The ads he took out in newspapers and magazines showed happy people saying the equivalent of "I think Hudson River water is terrific! I bathe in it and swim it in and drink half a gallon of it a day!"

I told Peter what we had accomplished with the EPA.

"What? How did you do that? Tell me how you did that!"

"Don't worry about how I did it, I just did it! It was done!"

The EPA waiver was the final hurdle, or so I thought. But Peter continued presenting me with what he saw as obstacles to the purchase. This went on for another year.

Meanwhile, the media had picked up on the fact that Peter Angelos was going to buy the shipyard, and a public debate began brewing. Peter's competitors and other developers realized they might want the shipyard too, and mud was slung. I hoped these local Baltimore politics wouldn't interfere with what we were trying to do here, namely putting 2,000 jobless people to work.

But the pattern of our phone calls never changed. As the year stretched on, Peter continually came up with a new problem that he needed fixed. Then, once I took care of it, he'd come up with another new one. I started to get a sinking feeling. I called my boss, George Kourpias.

"George, there's something wrong here," I told him. "He's not embracing the deal! He's creating all these fires that I have to keep putting out."

George asked me what I wanted to do.

"Let's look for other investors. Just in case."

The union put its feelers out while I went back to deal with Peter.

As we were nearing completion, the final piece of the puzzle for me was to put together a negotiated package with the final contracts for all the incoming workers. Peter's last ask was for me to rewrite the agreement that he had reached with the local district lodge. But the details he proposed were improper and I told him that it was bordering on illegal. He seemed discouraged.

The following Friday night, as I had expected he would, he gave me a call.

"Rich, I can't do this."

"Yeah," I said, "I kinda figured. You know, Peter, you could have done this a little bit differently. But here's what I need from you – please don't make any public statements, don't tell anyone you're pulling out. I need about two weeks."

"Okay."

"Also, you're going to have to take a lot of shit on this one, you know. The people were counting on you. Two thousand jobs, Peter."

"I know."

The following Wednesday, we made an announcement with the county supervisors and the city council. Peter Angelos was pulling out of the deal, but we had successfully found another buyer, Baltimore Marine Industries.

Like I said, throughout that entire ordeal, Peter and I never met in person. But I did run into him some years later in D.C. I was at the Hart Senate Office Building, attending a reception for a senator, and in walks Peter Angelos. I approached him, stuck out my hand, and said, "Hi, I'm Rich Michalski."

"You're Rich Michalski?!" he said with a big smile. "I always wondered what happened to you! You know what? Let's get out of here, let's go out to dinner. You and me. Let's go."

I suggested we go to the Monocle restaurant, which was just two blocks away. I knew the management, and it was a great place. Only when we got there did I realize the coincidence that Peter was Greek and the manager of the restaurant, Nick, was also Greek. As we stepped inside, we could see the excitement in Nick's face.

"Peter Angelos!" he gasped. "Rich! You brought Peter Angelos here!"

"Yes, I did," I said.

Nick and Peter spoke to each other in Greek for a bit, then we sat down and had an excellent dinner. At one point, when Peter went to the bathroom, Nick came over and said, "Rich! He speaks good Greek! Really good Greek!" He was just beside himself with joy.

At the end of the meal, Peter said, "Listen, Rich, I want you to call if you ever need my box at Oriole Stadium for any game or any event going on there. If you ever need seats, don't hesitate to call, please."

It was a sweet ending to an agonizing affair.

# Walking for Cesar

When the United Farm Workers (UFM) union leader Cesar Chavez died in 1993, I was one of the pallbearers. We did a 7-mile march in Del Llano, California on April 30, all of us wearing suits and carrying his casket, a heavy pine box, on a day that was over a hundred degrees. It wasn't easy.

Every civil rights leader from around the world was there. On one hand, it was one of my greatest honors to be a part of it. On the other hand, I got heatstroke and was sick for weeks afterwards. The weighty casket had three long 2x4s on each side, requiring three pallbearers on each, adding up to a grand total of eighteen people carrying the casket at once. Because of the heat, the eighteen pallbearers rotated in and out. In total, hundreds of pallbearers carried the coffin for a leg of that 7-mile march, taking it as far as they could before they had to drop out due to heat exhaustion.

I was one of the six people in IAM leadership that rotated in and out as pallbearers. Several hundred other IAM members followed behind the coffin, in a procession comprised of no less than 35,000 people.

Chavez fought for people that had no voice. He gave them a reason to hope by providing a path to secure contracts that will benefit farmworkers and their families.

# Sitting Down for Leon

When the Republicans took over Congress in 1994, the first thing they went after was tort reform. The goal was to reduce the average person's ability to sue a company or corporation. Their tactic was to set limits that were so restrictive, a lawyer wouldn't take up the case. Whereas a personal injury lawyer would normally get between 30-40% of the settlement, Republicans wanted to dial that number way down to 2.5%.

Leon Panetta, Clinton's chief of staff, contacted all the unions to get everyone on the same page to fight this proposed injustice. His hope was that we could hit the hill in an organized fashion and do our best to neutralize the situation through lobbying efforts. He set up a meeting at the White House for us all to attend.

I attended the meeting for the IAM, and it was held in the Roosevelt Room, the original location of Teddy Roosevelt's office. It's filled with artifacts that once belonged to Teddy or FDR. It's a beautiful, ornate room, right across the hall from the Oval Office. It features several large photographs on the wall, most notably the famous one of Teddy on a horse.

We all gathered around the conference table, and Panetta came in. A very gregarious and good-natured guy, he went around the table, shaking everyone's hands and speaking to them for a moment. He knew everyone in the meeting. As he made his way towards me, I got ready to stand up and shake his hand.

Finally, he stepped in front of me. "Rich, how you doing?" He stuck out his hand.

I started standing up.

And that's when the chair collapsed. I wasn't yet fully standing, so I lost my balance, falling backwards onto the floor. People gasped. The chair was in pieces, and I was on my back. Panetta looked concerned. He reached down, grabbed my hand, and pulled me back up.

"Are you okay?" he asked.

Everyone was looking at me.

"I'm gonna sue the bastards," I said, and the room broke up in laughter.

The meeting continued. We made a plan. We lobbied this issue with gusto, and eventually we did kill the proposal. It got so caught up in the politics of the city that the Republicans could not get the cloture they needed from the Senate.

Decades later my wife and I ran into Panetta at the White House Correspondents Dinner and he told her the story of the chair with fond memories.

# A THOUSAND CUTS

B elieve it or not, the previous chapter included some of the lighter stories from my work as Legislative & Political Director. In this chapter, I cover the heavier stuff, the situations that all but destroyed the American middle class and took me deeper into the political arena.

The politicians were the ones who were letting it happen. Fiercely protecting deregulation, they made decisions at every turn that favored making money over their own constituents' welfare. We were losing this battle due to attrition as working-class communities fell into poverty one by one. What made it extra painful was knowing we had the people who excelled in their skill sets. We had the greatest experts in the world in almost all arenas, yet they didn't get to participate in the American workforce because all positions were sent overseas.

Washington D.C. was not interested in helping organized labor. But I hoped that as Legislative & Political Director, I could help make a difference.

# The Airline Pension Fight

So far, we've talked about two notorious corporate raiders – Frank Lorenzo and Stephen Wolf. Now it's time to talk about the granddaddy of all raiders, Carl Icahn, and what he did to TWA.

In 1985, Icahn launched a sneak attack on the airline by buying up more than 20% of its stock. TWA was alarmed by the move because Icahn was well-known for breaking up companies soon after buying them. As the new company chairman, Icahn reassured TWA that would not be the case this time. He told them he wanted to make the company profitable. Of course, that turned out to be a big lie.

A few years after investing in the airline, Icahn took the company private. This was the beginning of the end for TWA. The deal made Icahn $469 million, and it put the airline into a debt of $540 million.

The next year, employees were anxiously awaiting the TWA fleet to be replenished. They expected 100 new airplanes. They got just 12. The writing was on the wall.

Then, in 1991, he sold TWA's London routes to American Airlines for $445 million, which he pocketed. Losing such valuable routes crippled the company.

The following year, it went bankrupt.

Creditors poured in and ended up owning 55% of the company. One of those creditors was Icahn himself, now in a position where the company owed him $190 million.

His next trick was to do away with the company pensions.

We represented TWA employees – the mechanics, baggage handlers, the public contact workers, really everybody, so this is where we came in.

Our members at TWA were steadfast and tough to the core. They recognized that they were dealing with a ruthless, uncaring corporate raider. They did not let their anxieties get the better of them. We had meetings to discuss the facts, and the workers were very articulate about their needs and concerns, their main concern being that Icahn was destroying their futures.

He wanted to gut the pension plan, taking out all the assets. This wasn't a case of replacing something with something else. This wasn't a freezing of the pension or a rearranging of the assets or the implementing of new modern policies. No, it was nothing short of simply taking away everything the people worked for over the last 25-30 years.

Now that the airline was in total disarray, Icahn had stepped down as chairman and the new CEO was a British man named Robin Wilson. George H.W. Bush was president, and Wilson and I headed to the White House to talk about what was happening. We explained to Bush's team that we needed the PBGC – the Pension Benefit Guaranty Corporation, a government-run entity that protects people's retirement funds – to pick up the liability for these TWA workers so they could still have a pension, so they'd be protected.

The administration said they would help.

So, next we went to the PBGC and met with them. The IAM team was comprised of myself, the General VP and his staff, and our economist. The PBGC were on board. They set up a meeting with Icahn, who still owned most of the company. During that meeting we were in the background advising the PBGC on what needed to be protected, but Icahn couldn't hear any of it. Still, he gave a blanket "no" to each and every request we made.

The pension plans were drastically reduced, but the PBGC was able to protect them in their reduced state. The workers weren't going to get all the bells and whistles, but they would get a basic pension plan guaranteed by the U.S. government. They were also going to get benefits. We protected as much as we could.

Icahn, wanting his $190 million, met with TWA and the PBGC in 1995 to demand his money. He left that meeting with a deal that ended up killing the company for good.

It was called the Karabu Ticket Agreement, and it gave Icahn the right to purchase tickets for any flight that passed through St. Louis for 55 cents on the dollar. He promptly set up lowestfare.com and made a killing reselling tickets. This exposed TWA to a daily slow bleed of its economic resources. Experts estimate the deal cost the airline $100 million a year.

It quickly went bankrupt again.

By 2001, TWA was slowly disappearing. It was being cannibalized by American.

We decided that we wanted to see the agreement between the PBGC and TWA to figure out why things were getting worse and worse for the company. That agreement had been hidden from us this whole time. Icahn had gotten the PBGC to seal it and keep it confidential. This was unusual. Our lawyers put pressure on the PBGC to share the document, and we eventually got it. We then learned, with quite a bit of shock, that Icahn had struck quite the deal back in '95, aside from the Karabu Ticket Agreement.

The PBGC had included an escape clause that allowed Icahn to walk away from the agreement if he was ever pressured to make any payments. He could simply elect to leave the agreement without any financial liability. So, just days after he got notice that he would be required to make a contribution to the PBGC, he submitted written notice that he was terminating his participation in the agreement. He walked away with hundreds of millions of dollars, leaving the U.S.

taxpayers to foot the bill.

He had walked away from the company without penalty, and the company assumed all his liability. As I learned this, the PBGC team acted very contrite.

"We're sorry," they said. "We didn't mean this to be so bad."

"Stop," I told them. "True, this is not a good agreement, but you need to remember that you had to make a choice. You had to either let 20,000 jobs go, sending 20,000 families right down the drain, or sign this agreement." They looked back at me. They hadn't expected this forgiving stance.

"Am I not right?" I continued. "Don't think for a minute that this wasn't a noble thing you did. You saved 20,000 families. You should be commended for it. Consider yourself commended." And that made them feel a little better.

But it was still a terrible deal. Icahn had an escape pod that allowed him to shuttle away from TWA, which he did. Just like Frank Lorenzo before him, he skimmed money off the top for years and then left a shell of a company in his wake.

By the end of 2001, TWA had flown its last flight and had been absorbed completely by American Airlines. It was sad to see that happen. At first, one might think 20,000 members, on the grand scale, is not a lot of people, especially when they're located all over the country. But that doesn't change the fact that 20,000 people felt real pain from this.

Throughout my career, whether I've won or lost the fight, something I've always endeavored to do is stand up and give a voice to those who didn't otherwise have one.

# Standing Up to Rahm

When Clinton became President Elect in '92, he started forming his Inaugural Committee. Our union lent the committee $100,000, and we gifted it another $100,000. Almost all organized labor that backed Clinton donated a lot of money as well. The Inaugural celebrations would last several days and end with the Inauguration swearing-in. There would be balls, parties, ceremonies, luncheons, dinners, a whole host of activities all controlled by the Inaugural Committee. Clinton's Inaugural Committee requested a meeting with all unions at the AFL headquarters to discuss how we could participate in all of the events.

Clinton sent his representative Rahm Emanuel. I had already met many of Clinton's people, including George Stephanopoulos, but I'd never met Rahm. There were a hundred of us in the room, representatives from all the unions of organized labor. Rahm walked in, only 32 years old at the time, and stepped up to the podium.

He addressed the crowd with: "I just want you to know that organized labor is one of seventeen special interest groups, including lesbians and gays."

That was his opening line.

*Well, that's fucking odd,* I thought to myself. *Why would he say that?*

It wasn't logical. We were there because we had earned a seat at the table through all our volunteering, hard work, and money. Whatever we were expecting, it was not that opening line. But he continued.

"So, you'd better cut back on everything you think you're gonna get, because you're not gonna get what you ask for. And you better understand that there's more people that need to be taken care of, and you're only one of seventeen special interest groups."

And as he continued talking, he kept repeating that one line, almost as if he were daring someone to challenge him on it. Everyone was put off, but we soldiered on. He finished his speech, and the meeting disbanded.

Over the next week, all the organized labor unions compiled their requests for the inauguration events. We put them together in one great document and submitted it to the committee. Then, we set up another meeting at the AFL.

It was like a repeat of the first meeting.

Emanuel stepped up to the podium, and in a condescending voice said, "I told you, and you didn't listen! You're one of seventeen special interest groups, including lesbians and gays, and you're not gonna get what you're asking for. And if you continue this way, you're not gonna get anything at all!" And the meeting adjourned. At the next meeting, we were supposed to present him with our finalized list of requests.

The head of the AFL committee was a man named John Perkins. He suggested we create a quorum of five people to go meet with Emanuel for the final meeting. I was selected, along with someone from the teachers union, someone from the communication workers union, and someone from the IBEW (the electrical workers). Perkins himself would come along as well. The meeting would take place at an old federal building right on the Potomac. D.C. is full of old, historic buildings that are really quite beautiful. This was not one of them.

There was a lot of old, heavy glass in the building. Everything creaked and clattered. It felt like a warehouse. The conference room had glass doors and glass all around, and we could see Clinton's team running here and there as we held the meeting. They were using this building to set up the transition.

The conference table was small. The three other union reps and I sat in the middle, while Perkins sat at one end, and Emanuel sat at the other. Behind Emanuel was a woman named Joan Baggett, a good administrator and a kind person.

Back at the AFL, we had bound all our requests in a book. Now we pulled it out. When Emanuel sat down, we placed it in front of him.

He picked it up, started paging through it, then closed it. He stood up, and he violently threw the book at the other side of the table, where Perkins was sitting.

"I told you," he said with growing rage, "you're one of seventeen special interest groups! Do you not understand that? You're not getting anything now!"

John Perkins was very quiet and reserved, and I could tell he didn't know what to do. I grabbed his arm and said quietly, "John, just let me speak here."

I picked up the book and turned to Emanuel.

"On the back of this book is a list of all the organizations involved. Let's just go down this list, okay? I want to go down the list on this book." And I read the names of every organization listed on the back, adding a short explanation of what each one did for Clinton's campaign.

Then I got up, walked over to Emanuel, and put the book back in front of him.

"What do you want me to do?" he sneered.

"Well, you've got a choice," I said. "You can tell us to get fucked and leave, and we will get up and go, and we'll be done here. Or, you can give us everything we want and say it's okay."

"What do you mean?"

"Let me be clear here. You can either say no, and watch us walk out of here, or you can say yes, and we can stay and work this thing out. But here's the deal – we want everything. This…" I tapped the book. "This is the minimum, not the maximum. This here is the bottom line. We've done everything this campaign's asked of us. For our purposes, everyone in this book is equal, and everyone should be taken care of."

There was silence in the room.

He picked up the book, then slammed it down on the table. He got up in a huff and stormed out, slamming the conference room door, which made the glass rattle like it would break.

His team member Joan then stood up. She looked at me and whispered, "Good job," then followed him out.

John Perkins looked at me with gratitude, and said, "Thanks, Rich."

The other three, however, were convinced I just screwed us all.

"I can't believe you did that!" One of them said. "We're gonna get absolutely nothing!"

"I'm gonna get fired!" another one said.

Then Joan walked back in.

"Rich, you got everything you wanted."

It was somewhat comic that for years and years afterwards, whenever Rahm Emanuel and I would bump into each other in Washington, he would slam doors, make noises, stare at me, and scowl.

This only helped solidify my reputation for not taking any shit from anybody.

# Gunning for Progress

With NAFTA in effect, jobs were rapidly moving out of the country. One place we tried to stop the hemorrhaging was in New Haven, Connecticut, where Winchester built its classic lever-action rifle and shotguns. Connecticut had already lost 90% of its manufacturing to Mexico, and the local union members in New Haven contacted us for help in 1995. There were two hundred employees at Winchester, all inner-city workers, and they were afraid they'd be jobless within a year.

We went over to their facility to meet with them. Winchester began making guns in 1866, just after the Civil War ended. It's a very old company. The building they were using in New Haven as a manufacturing plant was so old and multi-floored, it was impractical. Workers would have to load materials on elevators all the time to take them to various departments. Time was being wasted and work was harder than it needed to be.

We met with Connecticut state legislature and the governor and lobbied for them to help fund a new manufacturing plant just down the road. We told them it would keep jobs in the community and even improve business. They agreed to back a loan for Winchester to build a new facility.

Next, we met with Winchester management, laying out all the benefits the new facility would have and explaining how it would improve productivity, lower costs, and maintain high quality. They agreed that if the facility were built, they would keep the manufacturing in New Haven.

Next, and most importantly, we met with the members. We encouraged them to weigh in on the new facility, to contribute ideas that would make it more efficient. They gave suggestions, and we took note.

Working closely with the state and with the company, we oversaw the construction of a brand new, state-of-the-art manufacturing plant on the same property as the original building. When it was complete, there was a grand opening, everyone celebrating around the bronze statue of John Wayne in the main lobby. Thanks to our joint strategy, it was a terrific success story, and we considered it a crown jewel of an accomplishment. The Winchester jobs stayed in America.

Sometime later, when Bill Clinton was running for reelection in '96, I ran into him at a reception. I told him about what we did in New Haven. I explained how it was a great story, and I suggested it would be beneficial for him to visit the place. It was a brick-and- mortar facility in a minority community that saved jobs. It was a big win and something to be celebrated and lauded.

He loved the idea.

"If you need a formal invitation," I said, "we'll get that to you, then you can come and visit the plant, and meet the people."

He said he was in.

The next morning, I got a call from Doug Sosnik, Clinton's Senior Advisor.

"Rich, what the fuck are you doing?"

"What do you mean?" I asked.

"We can't go to a goddamn gun plant! He can't be seen there!"

Now, I knew Doug very well. He was a friend. But he was very upset, and he took it upon himself to tell me to fuck off with this idea.

Clinton had already passed gun legislation, and he had banned AK-47s, but these Winchester guns were sporting guns. They were used for hunting rabbits and ducks, not for committing mass murder. They were lever-action rifles. They were old- fashioned. And more than that, there was a terrific story here.

"We're not coming," he said.

"Doug," I said, "Doug, let me tell you something."

"What?"

"Fuck you."

Three years later, near the end of Clinton's second term, the White House called me. It was 1999. Doug had moved on, but one of the president's other advisors asked if I could arrange for the president to tour the Winchester facility in New Haven and to have a special gun made and presented to him there.

By this time, Winchester was suffering in the gun market. All the trade agreements Clinton had put in place allowed for the Chinese and other foreign governments to flood the market with guns for half-price. Everything we had done to make the plant competitive was being undermined.

I contacted Winchester and told them about the president's ask.

"Where was he when we needed him?" they said. "He didn't want anything to do with us. Fuck him."

I notified the White House that we would not be setting up a tour.

Sadly, the plant eventually closed. In Mexico, Winchester didn't have to pay health care, didn't have to pay workers' comp, didn't have to pay unemployment, didn't have to pay taxes for infrastructure. They only had to pay wages, and those were essentially 20 cents to the dollar. First, it moved its barrel production to Mexico. Then it moved the gun assembly to Mexico. Then, in 2006, the New Haven plant closed its doors for good.

# Becoming a Superdelegate

Whereas a party's delegates are selected at the state level, and they represent their districts, a superdelegate is selected at the national level and is "at large," a roving representative of the party. If that party currently holds office, then the president approves all superdelegates. If the party is not holding office, the chairman of the party selects the superdelegates.

In 1997, Steve Grossman was chairman of the DNC, and there were two open superdelegate positions that the union wanted to secure. Everyone internally agreed that President Tom Buffenbarger and I should go for the positions. We talked to Steve Grossman about it, and then a problem arose – one of the positions had been filled, so now there was only one open.

Buffenbarger chose to step back. He said he wasn't interested in getting the seat, and if one of us did, it should be me. We related that to Grossman, and he brought the issue to Bill Clinton. Now, this was after our NAFTA fight and after our strong objections to PNTR with China, so we were curious how Clinton would respond to the idea of having me in such a high position. There was more than a good chance that he would say, "That guy? No, thanks."

But he didn't. He accepted Grossman's recommendation without reservation. This showed good faith, and we considered it a very big deal.

We all attended that winter's DNC meeting in D.C. Grossman led the meeting, got through all the business on the agenda, then, just as he was concluding, he said, "I'm appointing Rich Michalski as an at-large delegate. *Sine die.*"

*Sine die* is a Latin term that literally means "without day," and it's used as an adjournment in meetings to indicate that "all business is concluded here, and we have not set a day to reconvene." The deeper implication, though, is that "today's business is unchallengeable." It's part of Robert's Rules of Order, the standard for most corporate meetings in the U.S. My appointment was inarguable and irrevocable. It was an honor for me and the IAM.

The great thing about becoming a superdelegate was that now I had more access to people. It allowed me to attend any DNC meeting, including the business portion of the meeting which would be closed to everybody else. As a superdelegate, I was a voting member at each of these meetings. I was now able to connect with leadership across the democratic party, including the largest sponsors and contributors.

As a DNC at-large delegate, I was appointed to the platform committee in 1996. The committee travels around the country, holding public hearings. I made it a point to attend these meetings because there was always a faction in the democratic party that would put forth anti-worker suggestions, sometimes not realizing they were doing so.

For instance, at one meeting in Cleveland, a DNC member stated that we should ban the production of F-15s and F-16s. To that member's sensibility, fighter jets were a symbol of war and destruction. To me, fighter jets were a symbol of the thousands of good people in Fort Worth and St. Louis, not to mention the subcontractors across the country. So, I offered a counterpoint in the meeting. I advocated for the workers, and I added that we actually need those fighter jets for our national defense. "This isn't about creating a war machine," I said. "It's the defense mechanism that protects our democracy and freedom."

At another time, some members in the meeting were up in arms about timber. "We should ban all harvesting of timber!" they declared. Of course, they were taking the angle that we were allowing too much deforestation and were killing the planet.

"Well, hold on," I said. "You have to understand that banning the harvesting of timber will cause fire hazards." I explained how, if left unharvested, the wood would die. It would become dry and old, and suddenly it's the perfect kindling for natural wildfires.

Those meetings gave me a voice that was heard.

# The Tanker Deal

Tanker aircrafts are planes that carry jet fuel and can refuel other planes mid-air. In the late '90s, the federal government decided it was time to replace the nation's tanker aircrafts because the fleet was now fifty years old. They were outdated, and they didn't match the technology we had in the newest fighters and bombers. So, the government put out a request for bids to build 100 tanker aircrafts for $20 billion.

Boeing and Airbus emerged as the two major bidders. The union lobbied for Boeing, of course, since it's an American company and the tankers would be built in Washington state. Airbus is a European company based in France. It was easy math.

Everything worked out as planned, and the government awarded the job to Boeing. Everybody was ecstatic. It was the largest military contract in the world and guaranteed work for decades to come.

But over the next couple of years, a scandal broke out, and everything fell apart.

Boeing's Chief Financial Officer Michael Sears was incriminated in a procurement crime. The Federal District Court learned that while he was negotiating the $20 billion contract with the Pentagon, he was also negotiating the hiring of that same Pentagon contact as an executive at Boeing. Her name was Darleen Druyan, and, through her daughter who happened to be a Boeing employee, she let on to Sears that she wanted to retire from the government work and take up a position in the private sector. Sears then wooed her with promises of employment while continuing to negotiate the tanker deal.

The judge sent Sears to prison for four months.

In light of the inappropriate way the contract had been secured, it was pulled from Boeing and put back out for bid again.

Arizona senator John McCain, with eyes on the presidency, went ballistic over the scandal. He always maintained that American military contractors were crooked. He took up a PR campaign to trash the Boeing program and laud Airbus. McCain's team worked with the Airbus America team, headed by a former test pilot named Allen McArtor. They led an aggressive campaign in Washington to win the award, and they got it.

Now Airbus had the tanker deal.

We weren't going to take that lying down, and we didn't. We made a formal appeal and fought tooth and nail over the next few years to win that contract back. My role here was to coordinate with Boeing and apply political pressure in Washington from various communities around the country. This was an all-hands- on-deck situation, and we met once a week in person to hash out our next moves. This next stage took several years, and the contract remained in limbo while we fought. Airbus could not start building the tankers until this was all settled.

One thing Boeing did was look closely at the Airbus model and find its flaws. They found ten things that were not up to government regulations, and they listed them out. We took that list to Congress. I also identified all the contractors that would be involved with the tanker deal if Boeing won back the contract.

I stood before the congressional representatives and gave them our perspective. I emphasized that it's in our national interest to build the planes here in America, I named who the bad actors were in Congress, and I named those who were fighting on our behalf. Then I spoke to the jobs.

I was able to list how many jobs would be provided in each individual congressional district. We could tell them exactly how many people would benefit if Boeing got the award.

Then I said, "Now ask Airbus – where are the jobs?" They were all going to be in Toulouse, France.

Airbus then invited me to Toulouse, to share their side of the story. I flew out there, and it was quite the trip. They appealed to me as a Machinist Union representative, telling me that they wanted to work with us, but nothing they could say changed the fact that they were stealing these jobs from the American workers. The whole experience had a touch of the surreal as we held our meeting in the boardroom on the second floor of their building, while they were firing the chairman of the board of the company on the first floor.

I got back to America, and we continued our campaign. We took such a hard tack against this that the government pulled the contract back from Airbus and put it out to rebid again. At this point, it had been about five years since the contract was first put out for bid.

As all this was going on, Boeing had been developing the 777, an enormous plane with engines that were 22 feet wide. One notable fact about the 777 – it was the first aircraft allowed to cross an ocean with just two engines. Before that, it was a rule that every plane had to have four engines to cross an ocean.

Airbus took out full-page ads in the New York Times and the Washington Post that showed both the 777 with its two engines and an Airbus plane with its four engines. The copy read, "Two engines. Four engines. Crossing four thousand miles of water, who would you rather fly with?"

It was trying to stop the certification of the 777, which didn't have much to do with the military contract, but it shows that the fight between these two companies went deep.

To address our point about not giving Americans the jobs, Airbus started to promise that it would build in the United States. We asked where, but they had no answers. We doubted they even had a plan. The company used smoke and mirrors in its communications to try to placate whatever seemed to be the problem without ever really taking action to solve the problem, and we called that out on that.

Throughout all of it, I continued repeating myself to Congress: "I just want you to ask yourself this one question – where are the jobs in my district?" I was a real thorn in Airbus's side, and I'm sure the company saw the IAM as Public Enemy #1.

I decided I needed to sit down and talk face-to-face with McCain's people. I went to his office, but they would not meet with me.

I kept trying, but it was a dead end. I mentioned this to a friend of mine, and he said he knew a member of McCain's legislative staff. "I'll get her to meet with you," he offered. I told him that would be great.

He made a call, got her OK, and gave me her number. I called. She suggested we meet in a bar.

"Let's not meet in a bar," I said. That just was not appropriate for a meeting this important and sensitive. I had identified the jobs in Arizona that would be directly related to the contract. Boeing was spending between 1.5 and 2 billion dollars on contractors in the state already, and I wanted to impress that upon her.

We decided on a restaurant in a hotel on Capitol Hill. My friend who had set up the meeting came along as a sort of buffer.

As we ate dinner, I went into my spiel. I chose my words carefully and I spoke with intent. I talked about how the job would last for 20 years and would open up great opportunities for the people of Arizona. I said it would keep people working, not just in Arizona but all over America. I told her I had a list of states where everything would be happening, including Arizona, and that's where she interrupted me.

"I just want you to know," she said, "that I don't care if your people are working or not. You know, a lot of people have been going through all kinds of things, my friends included, and they have to go out and find a job. So, why should I worry if your people have to go out and find a job?"

I was baffled by this, but I wasn't a rookie with this type of thing. I didn't let it rile me. I calmly went through my main messages to her again.

We finished dinner, and I asked for the check.

She suddenly got all in a tizzy. "Wait a minute!" she cried. "You're not going to buy me a meal! I'm not taking a meal from you!"

"Don't worry," I said, "It's perfectly legal."

"Perfectly legal? Fuck you!" she said.

My buddy, who had been silent all along, spoke up. "Um, I'll get the check," he said.

I felt bad about that, but it solved the problem of the moment. I got up to go.

"I'm gonna head out," I said. "But I just have one other thing to say. I've met a lot of people in my life, but I've never met anybody as angry, and with such a nasty attitude, as you. You really are pure shit. There's something wrong with you."

And I walked out.

The next day I was contacted by a local Tucson radio station for an interview about the tanker deal. In that interview, I said, "John McCain is more interested in creating jobs in Toulouse, France than in Tucson, Arizona." McCain got wind of this and went ballistic. It just fueled his rage against Boeing and other US contractors. The fight went on for years.

We reacted immediately to any distortion of the truth they put out there. If they'd put out an ad, we'd put out an ad. If they got on the radio, we'd get on the radio. If they went on TV, we went on TV.

Finally, twelve years after the contract was first put out to bid, Boeing won it back. We had done it.

As everything was being settled, I had a breakfast meeting with my president, Tom Buffenbarger, and the president of Airbus America, Allen McArtor. The meeting was called for 6:30 a.m. at the Mayflower Hotel, one of the most historic hotels in D.C. I arrived early and was just hanging out. I'd never met McArtor before, but I knew what he looked like. I saw him come in and get seated at our table.

I walked over and introduced myself.

"I know who you are," he said with a steely look. "There's a lot of broken furniture in this town because of you!"

"Hold on," I said. "Can you save that? Just save it till my

president shows up, then say it again. Please."

This victory felt particularly good.

# The Matador Cometh

The federal government sticks to two tenets when it comes to maintaining its own property. One is to buy goods and services only from America, and the other is to spread out the work so that all companies in each particular sector would be represented. This is true for everything from air conditioning to building maintenance to groundskeeping. For groundskeeping specifically, there are four or five different competitors, among them John Deere and Toro.

John Deere called the union one day to ask for help because Toro had approached the Bureau of Prisons to ask for all their groundskeeping work. Toro promised a very low price, if the Bureau would make it the single-source supplier. Toro's proposal was simply to close its U.S. factories and move its entire operation into the prisons. It would build its equipment on the prison property and – here was the core of the idea – use the convicts as the workers.

The Bureau of Prisons was not against this idea. The cost was temptingly low, and the savings would be considerate. To take this idea to the next step, the Bureau put out an RFP for the work. (An RFP is a "request for proposal," where an entity solicits bids from various companies.) John Deere was worried and asked the IAM to help them out.

I went over to the Bureau of Prisons, which is right there on Capitol Hill, behind the Hyatt. It's an odd place – very stark and antiseptic. They don't get too many visitors, and they were a bit leery of me as I walked in.

"Who are you?"

I told them who I was and what I did.

"Well, what are you doing here? You have no business here."

I told them I did have business there, and that I was representing IAM members at John Deere, and that I wanted to schedule a meeting with the Bureau of Prisons so I could bring some people from John Deere over to speak before the Bureau voted on the Toro proposal.

They let me schedule a meeting.

John Deere was sending their management team out for it, but I asked them to also bring a worker. "Bring someone who would lose their job if this deal went through," I told them.

Then, I found some sympathetic members of Congress, and we put together a campaign to lobby the Hill for the issue.

The night before our meeting with the Bureau, I met with the John Deere team. They were very cooperative with everything I was suggesting, and they were a bit in shock that they even had to defend themselves on this issue. I said, "Well, don't be shocked. This is reality. This is a challenge, and it means we have to win. So, let's not look for sympathy here. Let's punch back."

And the following day, we did. We were very defiant throughout the meeting. Finally, it came time for the John Deere worker to speak. It was a young lady who had three kids and no spouse. Before she spoke, I said a few words.

"Let me say something before this young lady speaks," I said. "If you agree to the Toro deal, you are unemploying this person. She has three dependents who rely on her for clothes, tuition, food, everything. You will be unemploying her and instead employing a convict, somebody who may have raped or robbed, somebody who most certainly has harmed other people. You're going to employ somebody like that and put her out of work?"

One member of the board we were addressing responded with, "How can you say we're going to do something like that?"

That opened the door for me.

"And there's more than just her. I have a whole list." I showed them my list of names. "These are all stories. Every one of these names is a story about another human being and another family, and you're going to wipe those stories out. The biggest violations these people have committed have been, maybe, jaywalking and speeding. And these are the people you will be punishing while you're rewarding the convicts. It's morally wrong. I'm going to give each one of you a list of these names."

We won that fight. The Toro proposal was crushed.


# Into the Trees with Weyerhauser

One benefit of the job was getting an education in all these industries that I didn't really know. As a legislative director in the 1990s, I represented lumberjacks. At the time, I figured I knew the nature of trees pretty well, but I quickly learned that I didn't know anything next to these guys. They were stewards of the forest. They lived and breathed trees. They were sensitive to everything in the ecosystem. They loved to hunt and fish, and they loved the land. These members and their families, as far as I was concerned, were true environmentalists.

One of their jobs was salvaging timber, which means going through a forest after a fire or disease had broken out, and getting out all the dead trees because the core of the wood was still good. The reason I was representing them at that particular time was because they were being accused by self-proclaimed environmentalists to be deliberately setting fires to get more timber to salvage.

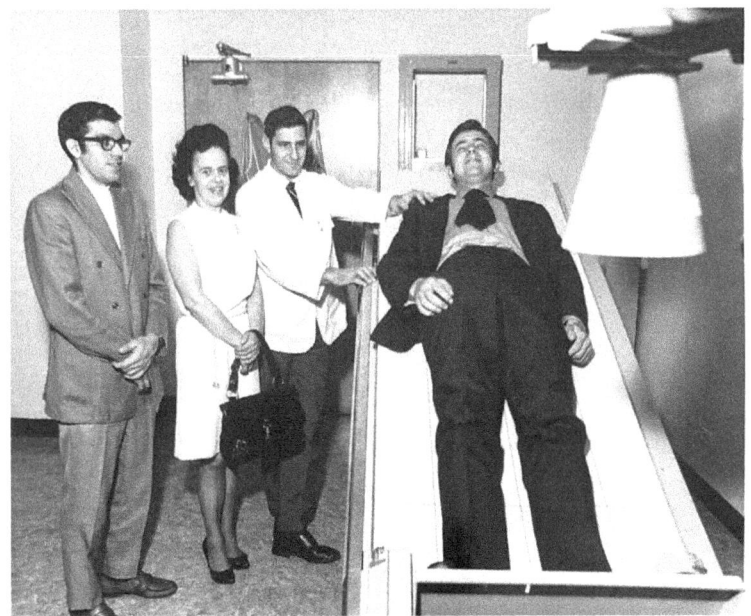

1971. Me on a GE X-ray machine.

1979. Pinning a "Buy American" pin on Ed Asner's lapel at Serb Hall
in Milwaukee the night I introduced Ted Kennedy at the rally.

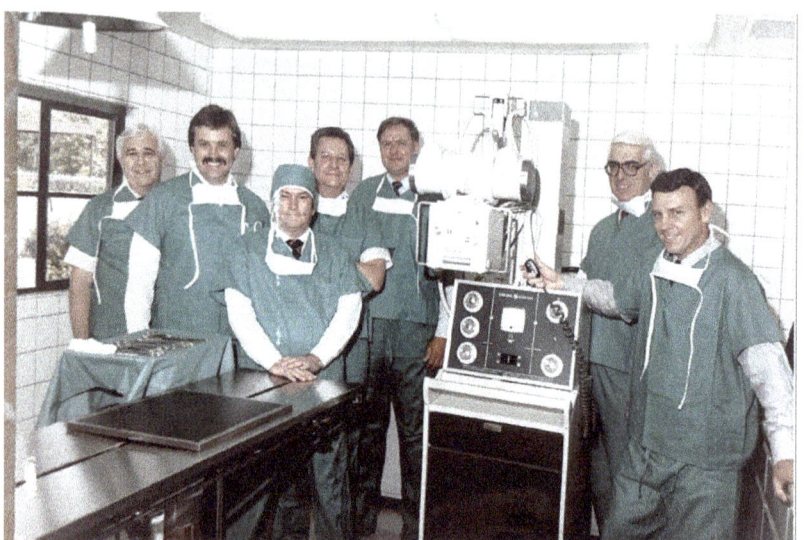

1983. Guide Dogs of America, Sylmar, CA. GE donated the X-ray machine and operating room, and the members donated their time to build the machine.

Shooting a video on the hill about legislative issues for members.

1985. John Trani in the center. He was President of GE Healthcare and later became CEO of Stanley Works.

1992. Legislative Director, Washington, D.C.

1993. President Bill Clinton, DNC event.

1993. Cesar Chavez Memorial for being a pallbearer.

1993. Wisconsin U.S. Senator Russ Feingold.

1993. Senator Ted Kennedy and his wife Vicki.

1994. President Clinton in the Oval Office following his weekly radio broadcast.

1995. Harley Davidson plant, York, PA. IAM President George Kourpias on the left.

**IN THE FIGHT**

1996. Texas Governor Ann Richards. She was defeated by George W. Bush in her re-election.

1996. Congressman John Dingell, Chairman of the Energy & Commerce Committee and the longest serving congressman in history.

Speaking at the DNC.

1999. Opening of United Airlines maintenance facility in Indianapolis with the help of Governor Evan Bayh.

Oct 2000. Running into presidential candidate Al Gore on my morning run on the D.C. Mall.

2001. The first UPS flight to China, from Ontario, CA to Beijing.

Apr 2001. California Governor Grey Davis.

2004. UPS Team in China to build a school.

2004. With a future student of the school we built in China.

2004. Congresswoman and Democratic Whip Nancy Pelosi, with AFL President
John Sweeney and his wife on left and Congressman George Miller on right.

May 2005. UPS School Building Team, Lipa Poland.

May 2005. UPS Poland trip with students from the school.

May 2005. UPS School Building Trip in Ukraine, with teachers from
the school where we installed computers.

2007. Senator Hillary Clinton in the backyard of her home in Washington, D.C.

2009. Boeing Plant, Everett, WA. L to R: IAM President Tom Buffenbarger, Boeing CEO Jim McNerney, me, President Obama, Boeing President of Commercial Airplanes Jim Albaugh.

Trap shooting political fundraiser in Maryland.

2011. Tanker Deal Award.

2012. Speaking to Boeing subcontractors in support of winning the Tanker Deal.

2013 Retirement party. Senate Majority Leader Harry Reid, my wife Nancy Michalski, and IAM President Tom Buffenbarger in the background.

Mr. Richard Michalski
General Vice President
International Association of Machinists and Aerospace Workers
9000 Machinists Place
Upper Marlboro, MD 20772

Dear Rich,

On behalf of the 5,400 Beechcraft employees around the world, I would like to personally congratulate you on your retirement from the International Association of Machinists and Aerospace Workers (IAMAW).

It has always been a pleasure to work with you. I consider you not only a valuable asset to the IAMAW, but a trusted partner of Beechcraft. Your hard work and diligence has greatly benefitted our employees and our company.

While you will be missed by all of us at Beechcraft, we wish you well in your future endeavors. Retirement will surely offer you many new opportunities, for which I know you will embrace whole-heartedly, just as you did with the IAMAW.

Please keep in touch, and feel free to visit us anytime you may be in Wichita. I wish you an enjoyable and rewarding retirement!

Sincerely,

Bill Boisture
Chief Executive Officer
Beechcraft Corporation

Letter from Beechcraft CEO Bill Boisture.

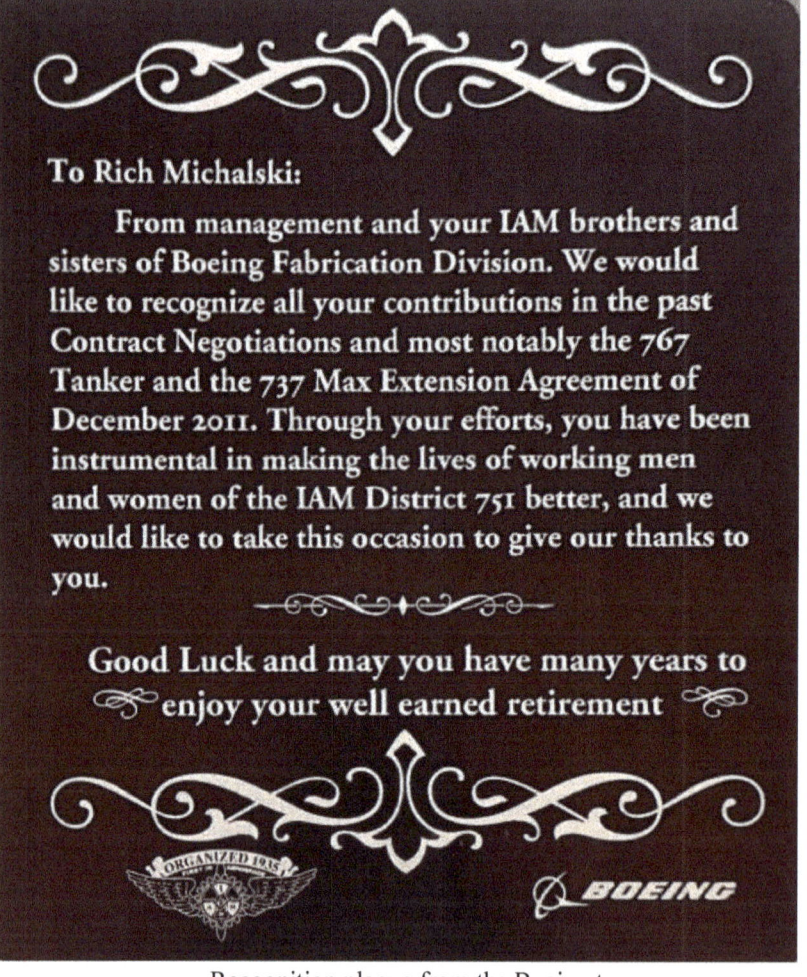

To Rich Michalski:

From management and your IAM brothers and sisters of Boeing Fabrication Division. We would like to recognize all your contributions in the past Contract Negotiations and most notably the 767 Tanker and the 737 Max Extension Agreement of December 2011. Through your efforts, you have been instrumental in making the lives of working men and women of the IAM District 751 better, and we would like to take this occasion to give our thanks to you.

Good Luck and may you have many years to enjoy your well earned retirement

ORGANIZED 1935

BOEING

Recognition plaque from the Boeing team.

Of course, there were some bad apples in the lot, but that was not most of them. By this point, lumberjacks were mainly independent contractors. Big companies in the forest products industry like Weyerhauser, because of the Reagan's tax laws, had to lay off a lot of their direct labor people in the 1980s. Those labor folks became contractors. While most continued staying respectful to the land, some became cowboys and just harvested everything they could find. When they'd get caught, the self-proclaimed environmentalists would run them up the flagpole and claim the entire industry was full of those people.

I represented the good ones and made it known to the government and everybody else that these people were doing right by the environment.

Later, I was on the board of the forest products industry council. We had meetings a couple times a year, and I worked closely with Weyerhauser.

The company CEO was Jack Creighton, the first non-Weyerhauser family member to become CEO, and he was a different type of corporate boss. He was a rare individual, a wonderful man. Exceedingly cordial when it came to how the company treated the union workers, he made himself available to his employees and he was very present for all the day-to-day work. When he stepped into the role, the company built a new headquarters (all out of wood, of course), and Jack's office was the room in the middle of the building. Anyone in the company could approach him at any time.

Under Jack's leadership, the company thrived. I learned from Weyerhauser that the forest products industry makes lifetime investments. It considers the results of its actions generations ahead of time. If they plant a hardwood tree, they know they're not going to harvest it for twenty or thirty years, so they have no choice but to think ahead and plan accordingly. "Weyerhauser plants for the future," is a saying I used to use all the time back then.

Because Jack made himself available at all times, he expected others always to be available to him. Since he truly believed that the IAM and Weyerhauser were real partners, he figured I could be accessed anytime. One night I was in D.C., the phone rang at midnight.

"I got a problem with these teamsters, Rich!"

"What? Who is this?"

"It's Jack!"

"Jack?"

"Jack Creighton! I'm telling you, I got a problem with these teamsters!"

I got my bearings. Jack was three hours earlier than me, and he didn't know I was in D.C. at the time. I asked him to explain his problem. It was a slowdown by the truck drivers. We dissected the problem, and I told him who to call to fix it.

But Jack was that kind of guy. It wasn't unusual for him to call and ask my opinion about statements certain senators have made, or any issue or problem that was concerning him. But he was not only concerned with his own problems, he wanted to help others too. He was very hands-on and sincere. We joked that he'd make an excellent boy scout. We even presented him a Good Scout Award during our IAM annual fundraiser. He was generous with his corporate contributions too.

Later, years after Jack had retired, the union was trying to help out United Airlines, which was in dire straits after CEO James Goodwin mishandled the 9/11 crisis and resigned. We needed a CEO to step in but wanted somebody friendly to the IAM. Because we were at the table, Tom Buffenbarger asked Jack Creighton if he'd come out of retirement and take the helm at United as an interim CEO while we looked for a permanent replacement. He was in his 70s by this point.

He agreed to take the job.

That healthy working relationship that I started with him in early 90s really paid out some incredible benefits 15 years later. This was true for so many of the relationships I built over the years. It was the long game. There are no immediate homeruns. These rewards are the results of years of effort. Like a tree, you plant the seed and nurture it, and after so many years, you've got something beautiful to harvest.

# High on the Hog

Near the end of Clinton's second term, I got a call from Karen Tramontano, the White House Deputy Chief of Staff.

"Hello, Rich. Could we arrange a tour of the Harley Davidson facility in York, Pennsylvania for the president?"

The Harley engines were built in Milwaukee by the steel workers, but the final assembly of the bikes took place in the York, PA facility, where the IAM represented everybody, about 2,500 workers. I was first exposed to the company when I was a business rep, and I had a good relationship with Vaughn Beale, one of the founders and CEO when I met him in 1985.

One thing I always admired about the company was the way it treated its workers. The company culture led to good manufacturing practices and empowered employees. As a rep, I was always demanding great benefits and the highest pay possible for the people I represent. In return, we'd work to ensure the company would have the best people and that they'd perform exceptionally. With that thought process, Harley embraced a new way of doing things. Management approached the workers and said, "Look, if you're a machinist, and you're working on this machine, making rollers or whatever you're making, if you see a better way to do it, or if you think different materials would work better, tell us about it. We're open to your ideas. Likewise, if you see something's wrong, or you suspect something is bad, stop the work. You have the ability as an individual to stop and come tell us." The company eliminated many supervisory roles and allowed the workers to manage themselves, including their timecards. It was a very rare thing.

Harley Davidson started in 1903, and it was run by the Davidson family until they sold it to American Machine and Foundry (AMF) in 1969. Unfortunately, AMF sidelined the brand and ignored investment in new product. The wheels began falling off, the bolts were falling off, and the company was getting equated with bad quality.

Along came Vaughn Beale, Richard Teerlink, and Jeff Bluestein. They wanted to save the brand. They roped in Willie G., a descendent of the Davidson family, and the four of them bought the company from AMF in 1981. They then came to the union and asked for advice to upgrade the facilities in York and Milwaukee. We advised, and they ran with our ideas.

The company began thriving, and they wanted to expand, opening another manufacturing facility. The union picked Kansas City, and Harley loved the idea. The IAM went out there, bringing employees from the other two facilities, and trained the new workers. Everything was working smoothly, and everybody was cooperating. The employees were happy, the company was happy, and the communities were happy. It's a great American story.

As Legislative & Political Director, I would always take care of Harley if they ever needed help in Washington. We had a terrific relationship. And the White House knew it, which is why the Deputy Chief of Staff called me. Clinton wanted a tour of the York facility.

"Sure, Karen, I can set that up," I said.

She asked if we could make it happen soon.

"Not a problem," I said.

Then I worked fast. I ran it by Buffenbarger then made a call to Bluestein. The company was on board. Clinton wanted to address the workers, so we'd have to set up an enormous tent in which we could fit a couple thousand people. We had to coordinate everything from the schedule of the workers that day to the timing of the tour to the timing of Clinton's speech. We also had to figure in the 60-mile helicopter ride from the White House. It took a lot of quick, careful planning, but we did it.

I called the Deputy Chief of Staff back. "Karen, it's all set up."

"Great, Rich, great! Okay, who do we talk to when we arrive?"

I laid it out for her – call this person for security, call these people for logistics, etc. She thanked me, and I finished the call with, "Okay, we'll see you there!"

"Whoa, whoa!" she exclaimed. "What do you mean?"

"Well, Tom and I will be waiting for you at the—"

"Wait. You don't understand. This is a presidential event, Rich. You're not invited."

This threw me. "What?" was all I could say.

"You're not invited. We don't need you there. And you don't invite yourself to a presidential event."

"Are you sure?" I asked.

"Absolutely."

"Fine," I said. And I hung up the phone.

A moment later, the phone rang. I picked up.

"You hung up the phone on me," she said.

I had regained my footing by now. "Why wouldn't I hang up the phone on you?" I asked.

"You can't do that. You can't hang up on me."

"Watch this," I said. And I hung up again.

She called back a third time.

"Don't you hang up the phone!" she exclaimed. "You have to understand that we don't need you guys."

"Fine! That's fine!" I said. "We don't have to be there. But I'm not gonna kiss your ass. So, fuck you." And I hung up the phone.

The next morning, John Podesta, the White House Chief of Staff, called me. He and I had a good relationship.

"Rich, what the fuck is going on?" he asked.

"What do you mean what's going on?" I responded.

"What the hell are you doing hanging up on Karen like that?"

"I'm not doing anything, John. Your team asked me to set something up, I set it up. It's all set. So, have a nice day."

"What, are you mad or something?"

"No, I'm not mad. I'm just not gonna kiss your asses. You disinvited us."

"Well, what are you gonna do?"

"That's just it, John. I'm not gonna do anything."

"Well, you can't do that!"

That made me pause. What did he mean? "What the fuck does that mean?" I asked.

"You can't just do nothing. We might need you. Can…can you be there?"

"Of course we can be there."

"Great. Here's the thing, though – you won't be part of the tour."

"Got it, okay. Fuck you. We won't bother coming."

"You have to be there!"

"If we're there, Buffenbarger and I will be there with the president, walking with him, standing with him. If not, no dice, John."

He had to go discuss it with his team, so we got off the phone. Later that day, he called back.

"I spoke to the president. He wants you guys to be there and to be part of everything."

"Then we'll be there," I said. And he and I launched into all the logistics of the day.

Everything came together beautifully. Clinton arrived and was given a nice personal tour of the facility with Bluestein and Buffenbarger. When it came time for him to address the employees, I went up on stage first to warm up the crowd. The company owed a lot to Ronald Reagan, who had given it military contracts to keep the company afloat in the 80s when things were sagging, so we were a little worried that the workers may not be so kind to a Democratic president. Happily, that wasn't the case.

They were excited. I stood on the stage and listed some of the great things Clinton had done that helped the company. They were getting more hyped up by the minute. I finished my speech, and we had a short break before the president got up to speak. Then the break was over, Bluestein introduced the president, and Clinton stepped onto the stage.

The crowd gave him thunderous applause and cheered like crazy.

Then Bill Clinton turned to me with a smile, looked me in the eye, and said, "Thank you."

Before the president took off, he asked Bluestein, "May I see the employee store?"

Bluestein came up to me, looking a bit nervous. "What should I do? He wants to see the employee store, but the ATMs are down. What do I tell him?"

I said, "Listen, he is not paying for anything. Give him whatever he wants!

Clinton loaded his helicopter with boxes upon boxes of Harley Davidson tics, no doubt bringing them back to distribute to all his White

House staff, something he was well-known to do.

# SPEAR IN THE HEART

Throughout my career, every situation in which I became involved was one of two things, either an instant issue or a slow, long-game threat. The instant issues were just what they sound like – problems that suddenly cropped up that we could then handle in fairly quick fashion. These usually ended in victory.

The slow, long-game threats were always strands of a complicated web, involving multiple factions and with the ultimate long-term goal of putting company profits over human rights. When these ended in victory for us, it was a significant win. When they didn't, it was a significant loss. These issues made up the war for the American middle class. We did our best to always fight for what's right, and what's right to us was keeping as many Americans as possible employed.

The stories in this chapter represent some of those significant fights. The almighty dollar continued to hold sway over the most powerful people in the country. Leaders in the corporate world and in politics justified their actions by channeling their inner Gordon Geckos. Greed became a force of nature, and humanity began draining out of our national interest like water from a sponge that is repeatedly being squeezed.

# Smoking Hot

I was on the board of the Tobacco Institute, a committee of executives from the tobacco industry and their labor counterparts. We represented workers at Philip Morris and Brown & Williamson, specifically the machinists that maintained the cigarette-making machines. Those workers who made the cigarettes themselves were represented by the Bakery, Confectionery, Tobacco Workers union. The Tobacco Institute was something of a defense mechanism. If the anti-tobacco movement released a study saying tobacco was bad, the Tobacco Institute would release a counterargument questioning the study. The Institute would also do its best to publicize the positive aspects of the industry, most notably economic benefits.

The general attitude from all these companies was not *we kill people* and not *we don't kill people*. It was more of a *hey, it's not illegal, so we're not doing anything wrong* attitude. At every meeting, they'd set out large silver bowls of cigarettes, so everyone could smoke as they talked.

My role in the Institute, however, was never to fall on the sword for the tobacco industry, and I made that very clear to them. I was there to take care of the workers. If the companies needed something that would ultimately benefit the union members or the communities, I would help them out. But I was not going to promote tobacco in any way. John Scruggs was the VP of Philip Morris, and I said, "John, you need to understand, we'll help you on things that are going to help us and help your workers, but your company kills people. I just need to be up front about this. What the company does is immoral. But I represent two thousand of your workers, and I'm going to do whatever they need to have better lives."

And I walked that line. I helped at the right times, but they knew

I would never advocate smoking. John Scruggs understood that, and he and I cultivated a good relationship. Philip Morris treated their employees exceptionally well and provided higher than normal salaries, and I respected that. I also coveted their offices in Washington. They were located in the Carpenter Building, right across from the Capitol.

As Legislative & Political Director, I was making two videos a year to communicate various events, fundraisers, and goals to our membership. The best backdrop for these videos was the Capitol, but shooting outside on the Capitol grounds was impossible due to all the noise. Noticing that the Philip Morris office was so ideally situated, specifically John Scruggs's office, which had a beautiful view of the Capitol, I called him up to ask if I could use it for a day.

"What? Why do you need to use my office?"

"Well, I want to shoot a video there. You've got such a great view of the Capitol. We'll have that in the background."

He sighed. "Fine. How long do you need it? About an hour?"

"Six hours."

"Six hours! Rich! Really? Okay. Okay, fine."

"And don't worry, we'll put everything back when we're done."

"Wait a minute, what do you mean 'put everything back?'"

"Well, that's the other thing," I said. Scruggs had been counsel for Ronald Reagan and had several Reagan photos and other memorabilia hanging in his office. "We'll have to take down all that Reagan shit for the video."

He sighed. "Fine, Rich. Fine. Just do it. I can't believe you." And he let me use his office several times like that for our videos.

One interesting thing about the tobacco industry – the companies had headquarters up and down the east coast, and the further south you went, it felt like traveling back in time. The southernmost companies created a culture akin to confederates during the Civil War.

It was like another world.

Philip Morris was the northernmost of the companies, and it was more on the cutting edge of the industry. It was the first of the companies to push FDA-controlled tobacco. The company then went on to purchase Kraft, and that became the mothership for a host of other commodities it acquired, such as Gummy Bears and Orville Redenbacher popcorn. Soon, Philip Morris purchased 40% of all the commodities coming out of Iowa. This gave the company leverage with the state government.

When I was GVP, Scruggs called me to ask if I could help set up a meeting with the Iowa governor Tom Vilsack. Philip Morris wanted to meet on some legislation that was set to be passed, and Tom Vilsack was the head of the Governors' Association, which was meeting at the time in D.C.

I scheduled the meeting to take place in Vilsack's suite in downtown D.C. I arrived in Washington the night before to go over the details with the Philip Morris team. When I arrived, the lead on their team, Henry Turner, instructed me to meet them at the office. "What? I'm not meeting you at the office. I don't work for you."

"What do you mean? What are you gonna do?"

"I'm sure you have cars. Send one to pick me up." And they did. I always kept my boundaries with the company, letting them know that I wasn't there to kiss their ass, and I never would be.

The day of the meeting, we walked into Vilsack's suite, and Vilsack himself rose and greeted me warmly. "How are you doing, Rich? Great to see you."

We sat down, and I introduced everybody at the table. Philip Morris had a team of five there and a couple of lawyers. When it was time for them to discuss their issue, I set it up for the governor.

"And now, Governor, this gentleman is going to explain the main topics here."

Henry began to speak, and the governor cut him off.

"Wait a minute," Vilsack said. "Before you say anything, I just want you to know why you're here. You're only here because Rich asked for this meeting. Not because you asked for it. I have no interest in doing anything for you. You and the people that you support with your money have done everything to stop me from pushing good education programs for kids and good healthcare for seniors. I don't know what you can say to convince me to do anything for you, but I'll listen to Rich. I won't listen to you, but I'll listen to him."

That floored everybody in the room. Nobody knew what to say.

I picked up the ball.

"Governor," I said, "I think what he's going to tell you is that they're not going to do business as usual. They're going to change the way they do things. He's going to tell you that they will support your endeavors and your goals. Isn't that right, Henry?"

This wasn't a set-up. The governor had taken me by surprise with his comments. I just went with it. Henry understood what was happening, and he played it right. He made commitments right there. After speaking about the issue, he added, "And by the way, sir, we're going to set up a private meeting with all our companies just for you, and we'll invite you to come and present your policies and programs to us, and we will work with you."

Philip Morris ended up getting what they wanted out of the meeting with Vilsack, and it strengthened my relationships with the company, members, employees, and the government.

# Progress in the Golden State

Through the '90's, Republican Pete Wilson was the governor of California and Democrat Gray Davis was his lieutenant governor. Over those years there were two pieces of harmful legislation that Wilson wanted to pass. The first was Prop 187, which he termed the "Save Our State" initiative. And from what was he saving the state? Immigrants. This anti-immigrant bill stated that if someone was not born in the United States, they would not be allowed to get a driver's license.

We knew we had to fight it. It took away immigrants' ability to participate in jobs and economic opportunities. It removed their ability to get to work. Many were union members. To deny them access to the job market was not in the interest of the communities or the state. We put money into a campaign against it, and we went door-to-door in a grassroots effort to get people to understand the issue. The proposal was inhumane, and all organized labor was against it.

We successfully killed the initiative, which set the stage for Republicans to continue to lose future initiatives in the state. All immigrants turned against Wilson after that debacle. They became 100% Democrat.

Pete Wilson was not happy. Organized labor had foiled him.

So, next he came up with Prop 226, which aimed to stop all organized labor from participating in politics, thereby rendering unions powerless. If the unions were forbidden to vote, then they could not vote against him. This was one we had to fight with all we had. I began flying out to Sacramento every two weeks to meet with the team we had assembled there. We'd get a report on how many California voters had been contacted about the issue, what areas were on board with us, what areas needed more convincing, etc. We continued honing that data, working on a weekly basis to get our message heard. I myself

132

even did some door knocking in San Bernadino and Long Beach.

We killed that proposition too. We beat them good on that one.

I built a great relationship with Wilson's lieutenant governor Gray Davis. Davis was very amicable. At one point, a few of us were meeting in his office about one of the issues above, and Wilson had just that day announced that he was going to move Davis out of the capitol grounds and into an office in downtown Sacramento. So, we were joking with Davis that he should make a newspaper event out of it by handcuffing himself to his desk and insisting they'd have to carry him out. He loved the idea, and we all laughed about it. (I suspected the lieutenant governor might have had a martini or two at lunch, the way he was so jovial about the topic.)

Ultimately, like many of Wilson's other plans, he did not successfully move Davis off the capitol grounds. Davis stayed there. In fact, Davis became the next governor.

During his time in office, I had two situations come up at the same time. Both involved angry environmentalists, and both required the governor's help, but they were two totally different issues.

The first issue was the County School Timber Coalition. This involved the harvesting of timber from state lands. The environmentalists were very much against this, and we wanted to show them that it could be done not only in a responsible way for the environment, but also in a way that would help communities. We formed a model that specified the criteria by which a tree would be harvested, criteria that promoted sustainability, and we relegated 25% of the revenue from that harvesting to go to school budgets within the county the trees were harvested. At the root of this deal, we were representing the timber workers at multiple companies, such as Weyerhauser.

We got buy-in from the companies and the county government, but it took some convincing to finally get the environmentalists to agree to it. But ultimately, they saw it was responsible harvesting and assured us they would support the coalition.

The other issue concerned a superfund site that Boeing acquired. The site had been the former location of rocket engines, and the ground was saturated with toxic fuel chemicals. The rule was that whoever owned the superfund site was liable to clean it up. Boeing was willing to clean the site, but the company was hoping to secure some credits from the state government for a bit of financial help with the operation. Environmentalists were up in arms over it because they didn't trust that a big corporation like Boeing would do what's right and properly clean the site. I met with them and talked to them about how it would play out, and how Boeing was going to properly restore the environment and, much like with the timber coalition, they came around, albeit tentatively.

Good. Now I had everyone's agreement on both issues, and all I needed was for Gray Davis to sign them both into action. As far as I could tell, there were no issues to prevent these two proposals from moving forward.

Then I got a call. Weyerhauser informed me that the environmentalists were going back on their word. They had met with Democrat Senator Sheila Kuehl and were pushing another legislation package that would kill the two issues we were trying to push. These were the same two issues I had already worked hard to get the environmentalists to understand and approve. But now it looked like they were submitting Kuehl's package to Davis's office instead. A few calls to my friends in Sacramento confirmed this was the case.

I decided to cut out any middlemen and take this to the top myself. I requested a private meeting with the governor. He was in San Diego, so I flew down there and met up with him. I briefed him on the issues, but he was already well-versed in them. I told him I was being told that even though we had an agreement with the environmentalist groups, they were still pushing something that would kill both items.

"Rich," he said, "don't worry about it. You got yourself a deal. I'll take care of it."

I looked at him. I had his word. What else was there to say? Would he turn around and backstab me like the environmentalists did? I didn't think so.

I flew back home and didn't mention my meeting with him to anybody.

The day of the deadline came. He had to sign any legislation that was going to move forward by midnight. Anything he did not sign would die.

I had a guy on the ground in Sacramento, and I gave him a call. "How are we doing?" I asked.

"Looks pretty good!" he reported back. After midnight, they would post the list of everything the governor had signed.

"Call me when you see the list," I told him. I was on the east coast.

At 3 a.m. he called back.

"He signed both of them," he said. "We got 'em both."

I could hear something in the background, and I asked him what it was.

"Oh, that's the environmentalists and Sheila Kuehl. They're pretty pissed off. They're screaming their heads off at me right now." He held the phone out so I could hear them better, and, yeah, they sounded mad. But that was a good win for us because it put forth good, responsible legislation that not only benefited the environment but also helped people in the California communities keep their jobs.

# To Lose, France!

Today, the IAM represents 525,000 workers. The union began 125 years ago in a railroad pit in Atlanta. A man named Talbot unionized the engineers who maintained the locomotive cars. They were the first unionized machinists. The Machinists Union has always been known as a "craft union," meaning the workers are more highly skilled than general laborers. They're multi-skilled. They're flexible.

Populated with 175,000 workers, the aerospace industry makes up a full third of the IAM. There are multiple classifications of jobs, of course, from the airline industry to the subcontractors to the space program to military contractors and more. It's very labor- intensive and very competitive.

It is also the largest single industry of value-added products that are exported from America. By "value-added," I mean that they buy materials from over 15,000 subcontractors, then they take those materials and combine them in such a way that they are suddenly worth more than they were as isolated materials. They are combined into components, which are further combined into products. By doing this, the company is exchanging value and making money. This is why the aerospace industry makes a good buck.

Led by Boeing, the aerospace industry exports more product and contributes more to the GNP than any other sector in the economy. Communities by the hundreds are tied to the industry's economic benefits and opportunities. A good example is Wichita, Kansas, a hub for subcontractors who build small airplanes and subassemblies for commercial planes. Those subcontractors make up the communities, and those communities benefit the local universities and trade schools, and so on.

In 2003, the Wisconsin-based premium airline Midwest Express decided to move from DC-9s to Boeing's new 717s. This was great news because it would keep many workers busy. The plan was that the planes would be assembled in Long Beach, CA by the UAW. A press conference was planned where the company would announce its deal with Boeing.

Then, a couple of days before the press conference, Boeing called me.

Our old nemesis Airbus had entered the negotiations, with its seductive strategies and undermining ways. Unsurprisingly, it successfully convinced Midwest to back out of the Boeing deal and buy planes from Toulouse, France instead. A new press conference was scheduled for two days later, at which point Midwest was going to announce its deal with Airbus to the world.

That gave me just a few days to try to reverse this travesty.

Since I'm from Wisconsin, I knew the local politicians. They let me know that Midwest at that time was asking the State of Wisconsin for tax breaks, including a "no fuel" tax and a list of other requests. When I learned that, I figured we could leverage the company's requests against them to force them to buy domestic. I called the president pro tem of the Senate, and I called the Speaker of the House. I also weighed in with the Wisconsin governor's office.

Each of them just shrugged off the issue.

I needed a new strategy.

I got a list of the manufacturers that were subcontractors to the Boeing Company. There were 42 of them in the state. They weren't big manufacturers, but they all added up to a key supply chain. I put out a notice very quickly to these 42 companies and let them know what Airbus was doing. I created some chatter there, and that chatter grew into a good rumbling.

Then I went back to the politicians, this time turning up the urgency. I went in person. I learned that both the president pro tem and the Speaker were going to be at a legislators' meeting in San Diego. I flew there and cornered them both, impressing upon them the severity of the matter.

In turn, they called the president of Midwest and let him know they were against the decision. "By the way," they added, "we're giving you all these tax breaks, and you're not even going to build the planes here?"

The president of Midwest was miffed. He then called the CEO of Boeing and said, "You can't do this, you know. You're threatening me. This is wrong."

When I learned that, I breathed a sigh of relief. It meant things were moving in the right direction. The politicians were turning the screws. Midwest was frustrated, but they were going to do the right thing.

At the press conference, they announced they'd be purchasing from Boeing. This was a good counter to the Jet Blue debacle from some years earlier, when a similar thing happened and Airbus won. This time, we got the jump on them.

After that, Boeing presented me with an airplane trophy that's the perfect little model of a Midwest airplane, and the inscription reads, "Rich Michalski – Boeing's Best Salesman."

# WTF, WTO?

I touched on this in the NAFTA section, but it needs to be explained a little more fully. Giving China the permission to join the World Trade Organization (WTO) was perhaps the largest nail in middle- class

America's coffin.

Before a nation can join the WTO, it must be given "Most Favored Nation" status. After NAFTA passed, the U.S. gave China the status of Most Favored Nation, and the country was allowed to enter the WTO.

The WTO gives big business a blueprint for how to conduct itself in order to save money on tariffs and taxes. It's a windfall for a business to receive that. It's a big leverage point. Once China became part of the WTO – China who sees itself as deserving special treatment, who does not see any reason to play by the rules of other countries, who only wants to promote its own self-interests – it began to hijack American intellectual property. It began to make cheaper versions of what we were making.

And the American public, very strapped for cash, began buying them.

We foresaw all of this. We raised flags, sounded alarms, tried to get peoples' attention, but nobody wanted to listen.

A good friend of mine, Kevin Kearns, was president of the U.S. Business Council, an organization with 2,200 family-run business members, meaning each of those businesses had less than 2,000 employees. After China entered the picture, Kevin's member businesses began closing down. They couldn't compete. He lost over 75% of his membership.

And there was one example after another of this same thing happening. I would take the owners of companies with me to the House of Representatives, and we would have meetings with congresspeople where I would specify, "Look, we can show you where China is stealing. These are the exact products, these are the exact designs. They're selling this stuff to the rest of the world and getting away with it!"

The congresspeople would listen and nod their heads, but

nothing would ever come of it. Sometimes they would say, "You just don't understand."

"What? What don't I understand? I mean, what team are you on here? We teach kids sports every day, and we teach them to play by the rules. Why do the fair rules not apply here? Where is the common sense in this situation?"

This all happened in the '90s. The 20-year-olds back then are 50-year-olds now. Back then, they saw their mother or father get laid off. They know their lives took a downturn after that. They know their lives are not as good as they could have been if that hadn't happened. Once-thriving Main Streets are now empty. They can't buy a home like their parents did. They can't buy a nice, new car. They can't send their kids to college without a ridiculous amount of financial aid.

They're angry. They're resentful. They distrust the system.

And what they would like – what they *need* – is for someone to make America great again.

Enter Donald Trump. By playing on that anger and distrust, he already had himself a built-in base.

# Daschle Threw the Snow

In 1996, South Carolina Senator Fritz Hollings introduced a transportation bill to Congress. Hollings, even though he was a Democrat, was no friend to labor. He allowed FedEx CEO Fred Smith to convince him to attach a non-germane amendment to the bill. (Non-germane means it is not related to the core purpose of the legislation.) This amendment was worded in such a way that codified FedEx as an airline. By doing so, it protected FedEx from ever having to be unionized. The company would be able to treat its employees however it wanted, it could cut costs wherever it needed, and it would have a price-point edge over its main competitor UPS.

UPS was a labor-friendly company. Because it was covered by the National Labor Relations Act (NLRA), workers had the right to form unions locally. As a result, more than half of UPS's 425,000 employees were unionized, and the company was paying the best wages in the world in terms of benefits.

FedEx, on the other hand, even though it grew into a parcel-delivery service, had started as an airline. That means it was covered by the Railroad Labor Act (RLA). The RLA forbids the company to unionize unless it does so on a federal level, meaning every FedEx location across the country must be unionized, all 290,000 employees, or none at all. Meanwhile, there had been some moves to organize FedEx in Memphis. Fred Smith wanted to squash those ideas right away, and so this amendment came along.

UPS contacted my office and asked if we could help. The company had gone to its local senator in Kentucky, Mitch McConnell, to ask him for help, but he wouldn't respond.

The only person I could think of who could kill this amendment was the Senate Minority Leader Tom Daschle, a Democrat. He had the power to do it. I gave him a call.

His office wouldn't respond.

I got some leverage behind me by calling the AFL and the other unions, getting them to weigh in and say, "Kill this thing!" I took that support to Daschle.

Still, crickets. I couldn't get in touch with anyone in his office, and nobody would even listen to us.

Congress voted on the bill, approved it, and made it into law. The special amendment granted FedEx the right to be union- free forever. As a result, since it had full reign to dictate salaries and benefits and cost-cuts, they now had the ability to offer consumers lower rates than UPS. FedEx stock immediately went up. This was a big win for Fred Smith.

Just a few weeks later, when the implications of this terrible amendment were still ringing out through the union world, we held our quarterly AFL meeting on the West Coast. There were about a hundred of us in a very big room. This particular meeting was attended by all the union legislative and political directors and their staffs. The key people were sitting around a large table.

I was one of those at the table. Then, who do I see walking in? Tom Daschle. He was going to speak to the group.

As he sat down, I stood up.

"Excuse me," I announced to the room before we could get started. "Excuse me, but why is he here?" I pointed to Daschle.

"Why do we have to tell you why?" Steve Rosenthal, AFL political rep, asked me.

"Because I'm a dues-paying member," I said firmly. "And I represent the Machinists Union." I turned to the crowd, who were all listening. "This guy just violated our rights and voted against us intentionally. He hurt a good union employer and protected a non-union employer. So, I ask again, what is his ass doing here?"

The room was quiet, and I continued.

"Wait a minute, wait a minute, I want to ask something else. How do you think he got here today? Did he fly in a corporate jet? Which company's corporate jet do you think he was using?"

Everyone knew he flew in a FedEx jet. But still, nobody really backed me up. So many of the other unions are in their own individual silos. The Teachers Union only cares about how things affect teachers. The Building Trades Union only cares about building projects. The Machinists Union, though, covers a broad base of members and craftspeople, and looks at the full communities that these jobs benefit.

"I refuse to let the meeting go on with him here," I announced.

I stood strong, and the meeting was cancelled. Daschle left. He probably went and met with other union presidents privately to handle whatever business they had. I couldn't control that. I could only control my world. And there was no way I was going to sit there and let him talk and act like he's helping unions when he had just screwed us in such a terrible way.

The AFL meetings were sacred spaces for me, and I had no tolerance for hypocrisy or wasting time. It was a place for union empowerment. It was our house, and I felt empowered to speak truth to power during those sessions. Sometimes Rahm Emanuel showed up for a meeting, and I did not shy away from telling him how I felt about his actions.

At some point after the NAFTA debacle, he showed up to one of our meetings. He was heading the Democratic congressional campaign committee, and he wanted to get some union money on his side. People from other unions, who had not fully grasped the impending doom that NAFTA was going to wreak, were thrilled that Emanuel was coming. "Oh, Rahm is going to be here?" I heard someone say.

"Wait a minute," I said to this person. "What's this *'Oh, Rahm'* shit? He just cost my union a hundred thousand jobs, how many did he cost yours? And you're gasping *'Oh, Rahm?'*"

At that same meeting, when Emanuel showed up, it was a similar scene to the Daschle incident.

"Excuse me," I said, standing up. "Who invited you here? I certainly didn't invite you. Who do you think you are, coming to this house, our house, when you directly contributed to the loss of so many jobs? We lost people, families were broken up, the welfare of our membership sank lower, and you fought for all of that."

My speech broke up that meeting before it started as well.

I felt like something of a guard dog for our meetings. I protected what we were doing, and I barked like hell at intruders who would hurt us.

# BATTLES WON, BATTLES LOST

After fifteen years of political and legislative fights, I was promoted to General Vice President of International Headquarters of the IAM. This made me the COO of our international president's headquarters in Upper Marlboro, MD, where I oversaw 250 employees who spanned multiple departments, including coordinated bargaining, legal, organizing, communications and marketing, and legislative and political. I had a budget of $20 million a year, and I was on the hook for the P&Ls of all departments.

The role came with a seat on the Executive Council, the managing body of the organization. I was also the gatekeeper to the international president. I had his back. We worked closely together, and my sphere of influence rose to an international level. I continued in my legislative & political director and lead negotiator roles, as they were encompassed by the GVP position. With this new status, my arguments had even more sway.

Becoming GVP was a huge honor. One exciting aspect to my job was that it was adventure after adventure. Once something was accomplished, there was another challenge waiting. It was 2006, I was 57, and I had plenty of fight left in me. I was seasoned, on my game, and leveraging all the power, influence, and tactical skills I had developed.

# The Asbestos Fight

In 1997, the Supreme Court heard the case of Amchem vs. Windsor, a class-action complaint where nine plaintiffs sought a fair settlement for being exposed to asbestos. The case had traveled up through the District Court and Court of Appeals and now was being heard in the highest court in the country. As a verdict, Justice Ruth Bader Ginsburg called for legislative intervention. She felt Congress should provide a secure, fair, and efficient means of compensating victims, and a Judiciary Committee was assembled.

The good news is that many in Washington, on both sides of the aisle, wanted to do the right thing. It had been almost a hundred years since the world learned asbestos was deadly, but big business was still using it for the most part, simply because it saved them a buck. They used it in manufacturing processes, in home installation processes, in asphalt tiles on the sides of houses, in floors, even in the blankets used to insulate hot ingots. (And by the way, when a worker would throw those blankets down – POOF! – asbestos would puff out for all to inhale.)

Asbestos doesn't break down and doesn't go away. If you breathe it in, it lodges in your lungs like spikes. As your lungs fight it, they create scar tissue. They continue creating more and more scar tissue until they stop working properly. It causes a cancer known as mesothelioma, and it's a terrible death. Like slow suffocation.

Asbestos exposure can also cause lung cancer, throat cancer, and other diseases. And it wasn't just workers who would be exposed. They would come home from a day's work with it on their clothes, and whoever did the laundry would find themselves breathing it in as well. More than 120 million Americans have been exposed to this deadly product.

The corporations continuing to use it knew what they were doing. People who worked in factories, shipyards, mines, and construction sites were being secretly poisoned with this stuff. Judicial hearings helped bring all of this to light. The good news was that a lot of good people wanted to do the right thing and create a system that would help these victims.

But the bad news was that politicians are politicians, and a large faction of Congress felt more loyal to their business supporters than the general public. Over the next few years, this group, led by Kentucky Senator Mitch McConnell, devised a bill that would essentially bail out the guilty companies and screw the victims with drastic reductions of compensation, cutting attorneys out of the process.

The bill proposed a paltry flat payout to all victims. It included deadlines and other obstacles to make it difficult to file a claim, and it put only a limited amount of money in each fund so that once it was depleted, future victims got nothing. In addition, the bill sought to make it nearly impossible for victims to find legal representation by taking the percentage a lawyer could make on the case down to 2.5%, versus the usual 30%.

This terrible bill successfully passed in the House.

Next, it needed to get through the Senate with at least 60 votes, a cloture vote.

Who was going to speak up for the workers and their families? Who would fight for *them?* That's when we were called in.

To me, this had nothing to do with union or non-union. This was about people. Yes, coal miners, foundry workers, and builders...but also their families and their communities. And it wasn't just a single community.

This was not simply North Carolina, or South Carolina, or Pennsylvania, or Michigan, or Wisconsin, it was universal. The problem was everywhere, and it was being caused by companies operating around the globe.

McConnell's group put out a media campaign filled with misinformation. There were TV commercials and newspaper ads claiming that the support asbestos victims currently receive from the responsible companies was unfair...*to the companies!* It was disgusting. The president at the time was George W. Bush, and his priorities were to the religious right, the oil and energy moguls, and big business. He had no problem with McConnell's bill.

The people who were really suffering from asbestos tragedies were the families because, usually, the person they were losing was the breadwinner. When the family's main earner dies, what becomes of that family? There's no money for education, for utility bills, for food.

Take that situation and multiply it by hundreds of thousands of people. It shows you what was at stake with this issue.

Money from asbestos settlements were mainly for the families, to give them a bit of relief after they lost someone. McConnell's bill aimed to put a swift end to that.

A representative who was fighting the bill called and asked me to fight this bill in a public forum. "But listen, there's a problem," he told me. "You're going to have to go up against the UAW."

The United Auto Workers were actually in favor of the bill.

I was going to have to fight a union.

Brake calipers contained asbestos, so the automotive industry was wrapped up in asbestos claims as well. All of these mechanics who were trimming the brakes, attaching them to the tires, or even just cleaning them, were handling asbestos. GM had asked the UAW to go to D.C. and promote McConnell's proposed legislation. Their UAW legislative rep was Alan Reuther, nephew of the old president of the UAW, Walter Reuther. I knew Alan very well since he was a union lobbyist, but this time we were on opposite sides.

But this fight was bigger than any personal targeting. It wasn't about beating up on people who were promoting the bill. It was just about prevailing. We had to make sure this bill did not pass. We needed the Senate to give it less than 60 votes. There was already a coalition forming in D.C. to fight the bill, and it was largely made up of lobbyists representing nurses, the medical professions, the HMOs. The medical industry was going to suffer greatly if this passed, having to treat patients who would not have enough money to pay their medical bills. It was an enormous, greedy move on the part of big business.

A key figure in the proceedings was Senator Arlen Specter, the former Attorney General of Pennsylvania. He was a Republican known for being fiscally conservative, and he did not want to put anyone out of business. He was a good man, and a longtime friend of labor. He wanted to find a middle ground. Usually, he was able to garner both Republican and Democrat support for his ideas. Despite battling cancer himself, he showed up for this fight.

I knew all the players, and I had all my materials. I was ready. The meeting was set.

The night before our first big meeting, I called the UAW. I wanted them to know I was going to be there and that this unfair, greedy bill had to be killed. I challenged them to stop the madness. "If you show up tomorrow and continue on this path," I told them, "we will not just sit back. We are going to stand up and fight, and it's not going to be good for you, I can guarantee it."

But of course, they were there the next day, and the meeting was huge. There must have been about a hundred people in attendance. Most of us gathered around a very large table in the AFL boardroom.

The meeting began.

Alan Reuther stood up and pontificated on the benefits of the bill. He namedropped a lot of senators, saying he had spoken with them and that they were all on the same page. Then he said he was speaking for union workers as well.

"Um, excuse me," I said, standing up. "Who authorized you to be a spokesperson for the IAM? Please tell me. I mean, do you know something I don't know? And what about everybody else in this room? Who appointed you – who *anointed* you – to be the spokesperson for all of us here? Because you are not. And I'll make it clear to anybody who asks that we are not agreeing to a compromise on this matter. We will stand tall and fight this thing in every forum."

And I did fight to kill the bill. After the meeting, I worked the room, speaking to as many people as I could. I kept the focus on people, not corporate finances. But it was a contentious subject, and both sides were equally worked up over it. We held another four or five meetings in the weeks following that first one.

Finally, the day of the vote came – Valentine's Day, 2006. My crew was not excited to be spending the day (and possibly evening) surrounded by D.C. lawmakers. "We're going to be on this," I told them. "I know it's Valentine's Day, but we have to be in the Capitol for this vote." They got it and I said, "Look, the senators don't want to be out of there for Valentine's Day either, you know? Remember that. I don't see us being there for very long. They're going to want to get through this thing fast and get out of there."

We walked over to the Capitol, and we waited with others in the vestibule outside the Senate chamber. It's a beautiful room with intricate gold inlays, mosaics, chandeliers, and gorgeous artwork. There was a mix of people for and against the bill in that room. I was dressed nicely, wearing a suit, and one guy mistook me for being on the side of big business. He came up to me with a big smile on his face. "We got them this time!" he said. "We're getting 61 votes and we're gonna win this. Fuck those unions, right?"

I smiled and moved on.

Inside the chamber, I knew Harry Reid and Dick Durbin were shepherding this cloture fight, while Mitch McConnell and his crew were trying to get it passed. The vote dragged on into the evening. Finally, around 8 p.m., senators started to come out. It was funny because we could tell who voted our way and who voted the other way by the way they'd look at us.

One vote I was sure we'd get was from Iowa Senator Tom Harkin. He was a great labor supporter and overall good guy. We'd traveled together and got to know each other. He would definitely vote to kill the bill.

But when he came out of the chamber, he walked right by me without looking at me.

*No, it's gotta be a mistake,* I thought. But then he turned around, walked by me again, and I could tell from the way he was *not* looking at me that we had lost his vote.

But at the end of the day, we prevailed. We only won by one vote, but it made a world of difference. Mitch McConnell's crew and the big business community were upset. It was a big win for the Democrats, paving the way for them to take over the Senate in 2006. It took momentum away from McConnell and pushed Harry Reid into the majority.

More importantly, though, this fight, and our win, benefited the families of asbestos victims – they could continue to get compensated fairly and without prejudice. Victims of asbestos had to go through a terrible and agonizing ordeal as it was, so it felt good to stand up for them and ensure they were still entitled to humane and fair treatment.

# Lifting All Boats

In 2009, the president of the Wisconsin AFL, Phil Neuenfeldt, who was also a Machinists Union member, called to ask if I knew what was going on at Mercury Marine, a boat motor making company that had two facilities, one in Fond du Lac, Wisconsin with 1,900 unionized employees and one in Stillwater, Oklahoma with 380 non-union employees. Only the one in Wisconsin was represented by the IAM.

He explained to me what happened. The company had sought a new contract that demanded certain concessions from the workers, including the implementation of a two-tier wage system. The workers voted against it.

In response, the company said it was going to shut down the Fond du Lac facility and move all its operations to the non- union plant in Oklahoma. If that were to happen, 1,900 IAM members and 500 management employees would be out of work. How could we get the company to decide to stay where they were?

The state of Oklahoma was wooing Mercury Marine, offering to pay for all the travel and relocation costs for employees willing to relocate. Everyone knew that the majority of those employees, most of whom had families, would not want to move. But Oklahoma was sweetening the deal so much, the only way to get the company to stay would be to fight sweet deal with sweet deal. The local union people in Fond du Lac had walked away, thinking it an impossible situation, and that's why my office was called.

"I'll talk to the governor," I told Phil, "We'll see what we can do."

I called Governor Doyle of Wisconsin and found out he knew about the situation already. But Mercury Marine was so focused on the Oklahoma plan, they were not considering any options of staying in

Wisconsin.

"I've been trying to talk to them, but the doors are shut," the governor said. "Can you open the doors for us again, make it so we can have a dialogue?"

I talked to Mercury Marine, and they agreed to hearing an offer from the State of Wisconsin, but we had a two-week deadline. If we didn't change their minds by then, they were going to announce the Oklahoma facility as the official plan.

I flew to Madison and met with the governor in person.

"The company will decide what they're gonna do," I said, "but we should maximize everything around them in this state so that it gives them a difficult choice. Let's make it hard for them to say no to staying."

We started talking, and we developed a strategy to sweeten the Wisconsin deal. I was back and forth on the phone with the governor's people, with my people, with the company itself, and we were doing all we could to secure funds to keep Mercury in the state.

This went on throughout the full two weeks. Finally, it was the day before the deadline, and I needed to talk to the governor one more time. I gave him a call Saturday night.

He had been presiding over a wedding earlier in the day, and he had participated in the party thereafter.

"Governor," I said, "I think we're close. I just need you to tell me if you've got anything left in the bag to help us get just a little further."

"Rich," he said, "Rich, I can't do this now."

"Okay, we don't need to talk tonight," I said, "But call me at 6 a.m. tomorrow, so we can have the final package put together by mid-morning."

"Okay, good plan, good plan."

The next morning at six, he did call. I had his whole team on the phone, and we banged out the final details we would present to Mercury. Wisconsin was all in.

"Here's something else," I said. "If they accept all this that we're offering, then I want the company to make a statement that they will permanently shut down the Oklahoma facility. We don't want this happening again, and the workers deserve that kind of commitment from Mercury, especially after all this."

"Oh, that's good," the governor said. "That's really fucking good."

So, we worked that into the deal too.

Now the deck was cleared for the bargaining committee to negotiate a contract.

Mercury stayed.

They made the announcement that the Oklahoma facility would be closed.

That was a good win. Today, Mercury is alive and well in Fond du Lac, Wisconsin.

# I Was With Her

In 2008, we supported Hilary Clinton. As a superdelegate, we gave her the union's full support. I knew her personally as did Tom Buffenbarger, but not as well as did my good friend Mark Weiner, who had known her since 1976, when he interned for her as she ran Jimmy Carter's presidential campaign. Mark was a stalwart DNC presence, but he was also the president of Financial Innovations, a promotional merch supplier. He and I rallied hard for Hilary.

She didn't win.

When Barack Obama won, he began forming his administration.

As Hilary supporters, Mark and I knew this was just a matter of time. "Oh, we're getting screwed," we'd joke with each other. "It's just *when* are we gonna get screwed?"

In January 2009, the Democratic Party convened for the first time since the election. This is when decisions would be made, teams would be announced, people would be reshuffled to suit the incoming Commander-in-Chief. Oh, it would definitely happen now. It was a week of internal DNC meetings. We just didn't know what day the axe would fall.

The convention started on a Monday. Mark called halfway through the day.

"Did you hear from them yet?"

"Not yet. You?"

"Not yet."

Was I going to lose my at-large delegate status? Obama's staff would surely not see any use in a Hilary supporter. Hilary, sure – she would become Secretary of State. But Hilary supporters? Team Obama would kick them to the curb.

Monday night I called Mark.

"Anything?"

"Nope."

Tuesday came.

"Did they get you yet?

"Not yet."

Wednesday.

"Richie, they got me. They knocked me out. But they said I can have all the concessions at the DNC."

If Obama kicked Mark out, there's no way I'd be left standing. To make matters worse, the DNC was keeping me in the loop on some backstabbing going on in my own union. My colleague Bob Martinez was lobbying to replace me as superdelegate. This same man would one day become president of the IAM, but at the moment, he was just a conspiring colleague.

The Democrats were not in any mood to give a machinist anything, but they were open to the idea of getting rid of a machinist. The fact that this young IAM rep was telling them that nobody would get upset if I was knocked off only fueled the fire. This was still Wednesday, but on Saturday I was set to attend a DNC meeting as a delegate. Would I make it till then?

Thursday went by with no news.

Friday came. I got a phone call.

"Is this Rich?"

"Yeah."

"Well, just so you know, don't bother showing up tomorrow at the meeting because you are no longer a delegate!"

I responded appropriately, though the words I used are not fit to print in polite company.

The usual course of action for these things is a little more formal and graceful. Usually the designated chairman would call, thank you for your service, then explain that this other person would be taking the position, but we've really enjoyed working with you, yada yada. They would ask if I'm in accord with all that, and out of propriety, of course I'd say, "yes."

But this guy was relishing his attack on me over the phone.

I heard him out, cussed him out, then with a sigh realized that I was out.

But I still had all my contacts. I still had all the relationships I had built. I was far from done.

# The Train Leaves the Station

Talgo is a Spanish train-making company founded in 1942 and opened in America in 1944. Talgo's presence in the U.S. expanded when it partnered with Amtrak in multiple states. In 2009 the company put out an RFP, announcing that it would give first dibs on building a train manufacturing facility to any state that was willing to purchase the train cars for use.

As it turned out, Wisconsin was that state. Democrat Jim Doyle was the governor. I had worked with Doyle on the Mercury Marine situation, and now he and Talgo were negotiating this train deal.

I got pulled in when I received a phone call from Talgo USA President Antonio Perez and the VP of Government Affairs Nora Friend. "You've been recommended by many people," Antonio said. "I was told you could help us negotiate this deal. Would you be interested in sitting down and talking about it?"

So, we did.

Afterwards, I got a hold of Governor Doyle, and he and I talked with Mayor Tom Barrett of Milwaukee and City Commissioner of Economic Development Rocky Marcoux. Our idea was to use the old, abandoned A.O. Smith facility right there in the middle of the city.

A.O. Smith produced the big blue silos you would see when you drive through farmland states. The company also built car frames, specifically the Fisher Body frames. In the '60s, A.O. Smith prospered so much that it hired thousands of people, almost exclusively from the local, urban community. There were about 20,000 workers, and they were all well paid. These were high- skilled union jobs. The surrounding community flourished when HUD started up the Section 235 Program, which helped gainfully employed people put a down payment on a house. It was a family- driven community.

Then NAFTA happened, and the company, like so many others, sent all the work down to Mexico.

People got angry. In-fighting broke out. Marriages fell apart. Crime began to soar in the region. With 20,000 people out of work, the area became dangerous almost overnight. Mayor Barrett leapt into action to save the neighborhood by securing money from the state and other federal entities to rebuild that area. In time, he stabilized it. But the A.O. Smith facility itself, a rather large facility at that, remained a ghost town.

Talgo became the lynchpin that would revive the community. It would build its train facility right there where A.O. Smith was and open at least 200 jobs to start. Our coordinated bargaining director negotiated a contract between the IAM and Talgo.

My friend Phil Neuenfeldt ran the HIRE program – Helping In Re-Employment. He was from my original GE local, and I had recommended him to the president of the Wisconsin AFL to run the HIRE program. Phil eventually became the President of the state AFL. HIRE was a program that matched skilled laid-off workers (including A.O. Smith workers) with companies who needed them. This was perfect for Talgo.

It was now 2010. The next gubernatorial election was held, and Wisconsin got its new governor – Republican Scott Walker.

President Obama, who was in full support of the Talgo deal in Milwaukee, announced that he was giving $800 million (10% of the total $8 billion Obama infrastructure package) to Wisconsin state to build the trains and install a high-speed rail. The rail line would link up Eau Claire, La Crosse, Madison, Milwaukee, Chicago, St. Louis – the whole Midwest. It would be a gamechanger, allowing high-speed commutes. Someone could live in Milwaukee and work in Chicago.

As soon as Obama announced this, Walker rejected it outright. He refused to accept the money for the state. It was part of a trend where

Republican governors were turning down any support from Obama for infrastructure.

The reason? Purely political.

They did not want anyone to witness successes under Obama. To the detriment of their own constituents, they were stubbornly doing what they could to minimize Obama's popularity. That was the whole reason.

After rejecting the money, Walker then cancelled all the train orders. Even though his own Milwaukee citizens were building the trains, he refused to buy them on behalf of the state, going back on the promise his predecessor had made and breeching a contract.

Now all those people that were hired were suddenly out of a job again. The trains they had built thus far couldn't be sold because the state would not take delivery.

Another part of the original deal was that we were going to build a service facility where the trains could be kept and maintained. This would have opened hundreds more jobs. Walker killed that plan too.

Talgo sued the State of Wisconsin for breaching the contract, and the suit was settled years later after Walker left office, leaving the Wisconsin taxpayers to foot the bill. Not only did Scott Walker deprive the Midwest of the opportunity to enhance economic development and have a crown jewel high-speed rail system in America, but he cost the taxpayers millions.

All those trains built by the new facility sat in storage for fifteen years until Talgo sold them to Nigeria in 2022.

# IN THE FIGHT

# FOCUSING ON THE FUTURE

Faced with some of these devastating losses, we kept the faith by investing in communities. Community involvement is necessary to be effective in politics of any kind, and relationship- building starts at the community level. The most rewarding part of my job was doing what we could to help as many local communities as possible.

One example is Al's Run, an annual fundraising event created by Marquette University basketball coach Al McGuire. We got some of the men and women from the Local Lodge 1916 to run in a five-mile race, raising money for the children's hospital. By doing this, the Machinists Union was recognized as a benefactor of the community. It wasn't a big thing, but it did matter. I learned that relationships with people and communities could be a source of alliance and support down the road.

I went out of my way to build relationships with employers also because it afforded us the opportunity to protect and benefit our members in the long run. Asking a mayor, governor, or senator for help bears more fruit when they know who I am, what I represent, and the community work that we have done, along with the presence we have in the communities.

The stories in this chapter illustrate some of the more charitable moments in my career, where I could help give back, be it through fundraising, helping communities, or laying groundwork for future generations.

# The 423 Building

I wanted to give the union a permanent presence on Capitol Hill so that we could lobby members of Congress by inviting them and the companies we represent to a private environment that we controlled. We could also offer the space to members of Congress for fundraising and other charitable causes. As it was, our headquarters was a full ten miles away from the Hill, at the other end of the Suitland Parkway in Maryland.

So, I talked to some people. One of my acquaintances was a Texas lawyer who owned several properties in D.C. He showed me a townhouse at 423 New Jersey Ave, just two blocks from the Capitol and the congressional offices.

Walking through the townhouse, I realized it would be perfect. We dickered back and forth a little bit and settled on a good price. At my recommendation the IAM Executive Council approved the purchase.

The address is in a residential neighborhood, so it had to be a place to live, not just a place for business. The basement was so cramped, you had to bend over to walk through it. I had it excavated so the floor was lowered down and the ceilings were nine feet high. My plan was to sublease this basement as a living area and conduct our union business on the upper stories. We ended up leasing it to a political organization. The idea was to make it expense-neutral, so that we get enough money out of the place to pay for the upkeep. The value of the property itself would rise naturally, which it has.

We knocked out the back of the building and gave ourselves another twenty feet. We had a wall built around the back so we could hold fundraisers and not be bothered. I also put an elevator in the building.

The union still has that property to this day.

If you visit D.C., right there at the corner of New Jersey and Ivy, just across the street from the UPS Building, and only three blocks from Capitol Hill, you'll find what's now commonly known as the Machinists Building.

# Building Schools with UPS

In 2003, UPS CEO Mike Eskew and VP Arnie Wellman called me with a special invitation. Once a year, all fifty-five UPS heads from different countries would convene in an underserved community somewhere in the world and build a school. A few members of Congress usually joined them. This year, they were going to build a school in China, and they asked me to be part of it. I was the only one invited from the labor union, and I was happy to go.

UPS never does anything without a plan, and they had this trip well-planned down to the minute. They gave each traveler a book laying out each day's agenda, to what job each person was assigned, and any other detail we might need to know. They also brought along a doctor and ingredients to prepare our own food.

The government and our hosts treated us like kings in China. The Chinese liked to see the American CEO and the American executives humbling themselves and showing humanity. It endeared us to them.

Despite having our own food to eat, I did try the local cuisine and became ill. Mercifully, it didn't last long. I was able to see the school get finished, and then UPS filled it with computers and other technology, including internet access.

Before coming back, I went to the markets in Beijing with my friend Arnie and some others. We walked through a street market where we saw skewers strung with skinned, whole rats, including the heads and tails! But the prices on the brand names purses and other accessories were so good, I bought a lot of them. And I mean a lot. I would give out these souvenirs to friends, family, and my office staff.

I arrived in China with two suitcases. I was leaving with nine.

Back in the U.S., a customs agent pulled me into a separate room. He looked around at the nine bags, then at me. "You left with two, you come back with nine. What the hell were you doing over there?"

I smiled. "Well, since you asked..."

And I pulled out photos from the trip. I showed him the school. I told him the story.

He looked around at my bags again. "Okay," he sighed. "Which one do you want me to check?" And he didn't give me any problem.

The following year, we did the same thing, only this time in a poor area of Lipa, Poland, located in the Subcarpathian Mountains, about 40 miles from the birthplace of Pope John. It was the same group as the previous year, but this time political analyst Charlie Cook also joined us. Charlie is a good friend of mine. For this trip, they put us all up in a castle. The walls of the castle were five-feet thick, and the fireplace in my room was big enough that a car could fit in it. The place was so drafty and cold, though, that I chose not to sleep in the bedroom they provided, but instead right in front of my fireplace.

For a couple of hours every day, we would go out and meet the locals. From what I observed, this was a severely poverty- stricken area. Many places we visited there did not have bathrooms. Most of the households had only one lightbulb in the house, though they each seemed to have their own homemade still. They would get snowed in four months out of the year, and they'd spend that time making vodka and drinking it. When we'd visit these homes, we always brought a set of pots and pans and some warm clothing for the children.

I was on a team with six other people, and we had specific tasks to build this school, which was going to be something of a computer lab. We build the entire thing from the ground up, starting with pouring the slab. It took about a week and a half. One team I observed was an unlikely pairing – the head of UPS Europe, who was a small-statured German man in bib overalls, and the head of UPS Cairo, who was Egyptian. Their job was to build the steps to the school. They had never met each other before, I learned, but the way they partnered on building these stone steps was inspirational. They worked together in true harmony.

When we finished the project in Poland, we then traveled by bus to Ukraine and worked on a K-12 school there that had no plumbing, so the bathrooms were outhouses. We helped bring that school more into the modern era.

The next school-building trip that UPS planned was to the Gobi Desert. I had a scheduling conflict that year, so couldn't make it.

The following year, they invited me to do it all again, this time in India.

"Do I need to get any shots to go to India?" I asked my doctor.

"India!" he exclaimed. "India? You're not going to India. I gave you the shots you needed for those other places, but you're not going to India, especially the rural areas of India. You have no idea how bad it is over there and what you can catch."

I decided to turn down the India invitation.

UPS continued this tradition to demonstrate that their leaders from all over the world care about people and want to help. All the people on those trips were top of the line, great people.

# The Big Boy Scout Hat

Buffenbarger asked me to do annual fundraisers for the inner-city Boy Scouts in D.C., and it became a tradition for eighteen years. We raised a couple hundred thousand dollars each year. All told, we raised over three and a half million dollars.

I figured we'd get the most buy-in from the executive community if we used these fundraising events to honor a person from government, a person from the corporate world, and a labor leader. That would bring supporters from all three worlds. Plus, it would be bipartisan to maximize the number of attendees. Also, to keep the message clear about who these fundraisers would benefit, I wanted the Boy Scouts to run the whole night's program. We'd start with the colors, the flag presentation, the Pledge of Allegiance, the Scout Oath and Law, etc, and then proceed to the honors. It would raise a good buck for the Boy Scouts.

I also wanted to change the usual set-up of these things. Typically, there would be a big sit-down dinner, then the whole ceremony, then maybe some hired entertainment. We didn't need to do all that. Nobody in Washington needed another formal dinner. So, we set it up as a little reception after work with hors d'oeuvres. That way, everyone could show up, we honor the honorees, make money for the Boy Scouts, and everyone can go home. That schedule appealed to the Washington crowd.

For the first event, we thought it would be a good idea to honor Phil Condit, the CEO of Boeing at the time. Phil was game. I told this to the Scout Master.

"So, I've got Phil Condit from Boeing to be the honoree."

"That's terrific, Rich! We'll present him with a Scout hat and neckerchief."

"Sounds good."

"Quick question – what's Phil's hat size?"

"Uh, mmm…huh." I pictured Phil. He was a large guy, bigger than the average person. "He's big."

"Well, try to get his hat size. It would be a bad moment if he puts on the hat and it's too big or too small."

He was right. That kind of thing could sour the whole moment.

I then began the delicate mission of finding out the hat size of one of America's most important CEOs. Do you know how many people are threatened by the idea of asking a CEO his head size? I certainly didn't feel comfortable asking him – it's too embarrassing. I solicited the help of those I knew around him, but none of them wanted to ask either. I called his secretary and pushed the issue on her.

"You have to help us with this. Nobody will ask him his head size. Can you find out for us?"

She laughed. "Sure, sure. I'll get it. I'll figure something out. Give me a couple days."

She came through for us and got the size. We all breathed a sigh of relief.

The night of the event, after the opening ceremony, a 15- year-old Eagle Scout stood up and spoke to the crowd about why he became a Scout. He talked about the things he had accomplished along the way, and he talked about his plans for the future.

"And what I'm really looking forward to," he said, "is becoming an employee of the Boeing company." He then pulled out a resume and walked it over to Phil Condit.

It was a beautiful moment. Phil was charmed by the gesture, and everyone admired the kid's moxie. Boeing followed through and later hired the kid to be an intern.

And happily, when the Boy Scouts presented Phil with the hat, he put it on, and it fit perfectly.

As with everything in Washington, you're always going to have detractors. Congressman Barney Frank was viciously against our fundraisers. He sent a malicious letter to the IAM president saying we should not be raising money for such an anti-homosexual organization like the Boy Scouts. "I'm going to break this," he vowed in the letter. "It's simply not right to support an intolerant organization."

He, of course, made no mention of the fact that earlier in his own career, there was a male prostitution ring running out of the basement of his house on Capitol Hill. In this letter, he was calling out the questionable morality of helping Boy Scouts. I decided to call Barney Frank myself.

"Listen," I said. "I understand this predicament that the Scouts are anti-gay, but what we're doing here is a higher calling. The kids we're helping are inner-city kids, many of them don't have fathers, and all of them are underprivileged. Are you telling me you're against that?"

I made it clear we weren't raising funds to benefit, say, the Northern Virginia packs, where the kids all lived in half-a-million-dollar homes. This was for the children who were suffering and did not have a two-parent household.

The congressman laid off his attacks after that conversation.

## Goats for the Old Goat

White House Correspondent Ellen Ratner is an old friend of mine. She would come out to our training facility in Southern Maryland once a year for a week to teach union members how to speak on the radio or on TV, in case they were ever interviewed. She would train them how to effectively communicate, and she explained the nuanced differences between radio and TV.

She ran a company called Talk Media News, and she had coveted press property on Capitol Hill, the Pentagon, and the White House. That meant that after sitting or standing for a press conference, she always had a little nearby cubby of her own where she could write up her report while the news was still fresh. She created news content and sold it to radio stations around the world.

Ellen had a passion: helping the people of South Sudan.

South Sudan is a very poor, primarily Christian state where many families live in tents and there is little to no running water. Muslims from the north would ravage these Christian towns, raping and kidnapping women. Polio is rampant there, and much of the population has been stricken with it, taking away the use of their legs. There are few schools, and only two or three medical doctors for the whole country.

Ellen had traveled there, seen the situation, and felt it break her heart. She knew she needed to help those families somehow and some way.

One thing she noticed was that there was a key difference between the families that were surviving and the families that were struggling – a single goat. Having a goat was a resource. It could provide the family with milk, as well as all the byproducts like cheese and whey. Ellen noticed that owning a goat was life-changing for a family. It was not just a source of wealth and health, it kept them alive.

She started a nonprofit called Goats for the Old Goat (she was the "Old Goat"), and she asked me if I could use my contacts in the corporate world to raise money to buy goats for these families. I told her I was happy to help. She invited me to travel with her to South Sudan. I said, "No thanks," but reiterated that I was happy to raise money for her cause.

The IAM sponsored a fundraiser at the 423 building in Washington, D.C. To remind everyone why we were there, I found a local 4-H Club in southern Maryland that had kids who raised goats, and I paid for one to be brought to the event.

I had no idea how ga-ga all these corporate executives and CEOs would get over having their photo taken with a goat. It was hilarious. Assistants were calling me every few minutes to confirm that their bosses would be able to take their picture with the goat. At the event itself, there was an endless line as company executives waited for their photo op. The goat was a star. The fundraiser was a success. We raised close to $50,000.

I did it again for Ellen the following year, and then again every year for the next 10 years. Each year, we'd make somewhere between $25,000 and $50,000. Ellen used the money wisely. There were other organizations that would raise money for goats in South Sudan, but they'd be paying about $150 a goat, figuring in their overhead, travel costs, and whatever. Ellen found local farmers in Africa and delivered the goats directly from them for only $70. She didn't figure in any overhead. All the money went to the people of South Sudan.

When she'd provide a goat to a family, she would have a photo taken of the goat with that family, and she would send it to the donor, so they could see exactly where their money went. When she found she had excess money from the fundraisers, she would put all of that into the South Sudan communities as well.

She built schools.

She built hospitals.

She bought special bicycles modified to be powered with your hands for the people who had polio.

She built a big community center and health care facility.

She adopted a 9-year-old boy and brought him back with her. The boy had been blinded by torturers who rubbed hot peppers on his eyes, just for being Christian.

She started recruiting people from the region, training them in a skill, and sending them back to help others.

Unfortunately, the South Sudanese environment continued to destabilize more and more. Ellen was eventually advised by the state department not to return to South Sudan. As a fairly wealthy Jew, she was in danger of being kidnapped and ransomed.

That broke her heart all over again.

Meeting amazing, inspiring people like Ellen was really the greatest gift my career gave me. At a time when I was witnessing so many people falling into the immorality of greed, it was uplifting and revitalizing to realize there were still good people in the world, with their hearts in the right place.

# IN THE FIGHT

# THE INTERNATIONAL

Negotiations between the workers and the Boeing company had been challenging for decades. Everything finally came to a head in 2008 – a strike that would last for almost 60 days.

The trouble started when the president of Boeing Commercial (BCA) Scott Carson decided to put some pressure on the union by using the media. Two weeks before the latest contract expired, Carson and his team ran TV and radio spots pressuring union officers to agree to the company's newest – and grossly unsatisfactory – offer. The spots ran in Puget Sound, Oregon, and Wichita, and their purpose was obviously to destabilize union leadership.

The plan backfired. Instead of changing minds, Carson's campaign put everyone on a collision course straight to the strike.

Scott Carson had been with the company forever. He collected Ford Mustangs. But as cool as his car collection was, his negotiating skills were woefully misguided. The basic rule of bargaining is to do it at a table, face-to-face, and leave the media out of it. The media polarizes people. It oversimplifies issues and reduces them to "right" and "wrong." This locks them that way in the public eye, causing people to choose one side or the other and then stay frozen in that position. It obliterates the use of nuance, which is a key factor in every negotiation.

Meanwhile, the community was already angry and nervous that Boeing had been increasingly outsourcing. For the 787 Dreamliner, management had outsourced thousands of components to outside vendors rather than manufacture and control it all in- house. This resulted in a delayed delivery of parts, which caused major manufacturing delays. It was no fault of the engineers, machinists, or any of the workers – this was the outsourcing, plain and simple.

With the 2008 recession taking a toll everywhere you looked, union workers suddenly, and understandably, wanted job security. While they were at it, they also wanted a fairer wage.

The offer Boeing brought to the table was terrible. Their "take it or leave it" attitude only made things worse. Negotiations went downhill from there. Some believed the company was trying to force a strike, so they could use it as a scapegoat to cover up all the problems caused by their outsourcing deals. The company's "best and final" offer to the workers was ultimately so insulting that in early September 2008, the IAM workers across every Boeing facility went on strike.

All 27,000.

The strike lingered on and on, and everyone lost money. The company was losing $100 million every day that their planes were not being built, and the workers were losing thousands of paycheck dollars. Nobody was in a good mood, and the contention got more toxic. We decided to bring the company and the union together for some federal mediation in Washington D.C.

Boeing sent their executives, but much to my dismay, they didn't seem to be taking the matter very seriously. Some of them snuck out to watch football. Carson himself came to town for it, but he only attended the first and last days of the talks. A core few of us negotiated day and night through that entire week, usually until 2 a.m. While we did have federal mediators there, George W. Bush's appointed Director of Federal Mediation didn't show up.

We called and insisted that he attend. This was an urgent matter, and we needed the biggest players to be involved.

Finally, on Day 2 or Day 3, the Director did show up. He walked into the room carrying a little poodle, of all things.

None of us were prepared for this nonsense.

As soon as he put the dog down on the floor, it started barking at everyone. It even scampered over and started growling and pulling on the pant leg of a member of our team.

"He can't be left home alone," the Director told us, as though we were all amused. We weren't.

"Let me tell you something," I said. "You need to keep that dog away from us because I will punt it right through that window."

"You wouldn't do that…would you?" he asked.

"Yeah. I would do that," I said. "I would absolutely do that."

The talks continued without the dog. It didn't feel like we were getting anywhere though. The Director of Federal Mediation tried to put an end to it all by gathering all the union reps into a room and telling us, "Look, that's it. The company's all done. They're all in. You need to accept their final offer because that's the best you're going to get."

He expected us to admit defeat. He expected us to believe we had no choice but to say "okay."

That didn't happen.

"All right, that's fine," I said, standing up. "We're done here. We'll leave right now. See you at Christmas."

And we walked out.

It was obvious the Director was not a neutral party. He was carrying water for the company.

*They're all in.* I couldn't believe he said that. It was clear he didn't understand the issues at play, and he had no appreciation for how far down the road of the negotiation process we had come. The details on the table were very nuanced by this point. We were working with surgical precision, while he tried to end the matter with a dull axe.

My team stayed up until 3 a.m. that night, strategizing our next move. The IAM was under tremendous pressure from politicians to end this marathon strike, and we needed a plan. We came up with our bottom line for each category of the agreement. The next day, we got the company and union together one last time.

The Boeing rep and I sat directly across from each other, no table between us.

My team sat behind me. The Boeing team sat behind him.

Minute-takers sat on either side.

The federal mediators stood nearby, watching and listening.

Our conversation this time was short and to the point. We ran through the issues. We worked down the list and got tentative agreements to each category.

Scott Carson asked, "Do we have an agreement?"

"We need something else," I said. "A $10,000 signing bonus." I explained that after so much time away, after so much lost in wages, the community needed this. It would show them that the war was over. It would be a step in the right direction for everyone involved. It would be an act of good faith that we're putting the strike behind us and looking now to the future.

He and his team left the room. They returned minutes later. Carson sat before me and asked, "If we agree to this, do we have a deal?"

"Yes, but there's one more thing," I said. Then I pushed hard for every worker to receive the $10,000 bonus upon their return to the plant.

As I explained my reasoning, someone on the Boeing side shouted, "No way! We're not doing that!"

"Shut up!" Carson snapped at the guy. "Rich is talking. Let him finish."

I finished explaining, and Carson liked the idea. But he added that cutting $10,000 checks for almost 30,000 people would take some time. The high numbers would tie it up in bureaucracy.

"Okay, then I'll tell you what," I said. "Let's do this – give everyone a $5,000 check the first day back at work. Have the supervisors standing there, ready to hand it to each worker as they arrive. It'll be a bond of friendship. We'll tell them another $5,000 is going to follow soon after."

He looked at me, weighing it.

He nodded. "Done," he said.

We stood up. We shook hands.

We had a deal.


Our members voted in favor of it, and after eight long weeks, the strike was finally over. It had been the longest union strike at Boeing in over 20 years. We were all exhausted. Happy, but exhausted. I felt proud that we got through it successfully. It had been such a grueling experience, we were sure that was the worst it would ever get.

We couldn't have been more wrong.


Everything was fine for a few months, but Boeing had left the bargaining table with a bad taste in its mouth. Company leadership still felt stung by the strike. They had agreed to the deal, but resentfully. They began complaining that the 59-day strike had reduced revenue by $4.3 billion. We knew they were lumping their own quality problems from outsourcing and the delays from their suppliers and sub-contractors into that number.

While they had outsourced the parts, the assembly of the 787 Dreamliner occurred in Washington, thanks to all the tax breaks granted by the governor. It was a successful plane and won engineering awards. The company wanted to increase production capacity and build a second line either in the Puget Sound or on a greenfield site free from the IAM. (A "greenfield site" means a new facility in a new location out of state, employing non-union workers.)

The company made this announcement publicly. It shocked everyone in the Puget Sound including leadership, politicians, and all the individuals that helped develop the 787 program over the years. Everyone asked, "How can this be? The governor and state legislature granted a deal with huge tax breaks for Boeing to develop the 787 line!"

My first action was to call Governor Christine Gregoire and so I could see the agreement with Boeing.

The governor was stunned as well. She was under the impression that her deal with the company was to build *all* the 787s in Washington. Looking closer at the deal, we learned that the governor's chief of staff, who had negotiated the first line of 787s with Boeing, had allowed in loopholes that let the company build the second line somewhere else. This deal would never have been approved by the governor nor the legislature if they had known it was only for the first line.

I remember wishing that Governor Gregoire would have made a strong statement at the time of the announcement, reminding the company there would not have been a first 787 line without the state's tax breaks. I wished she had remarked that the deal she had made with the company was not simply to build the first line of 787s in Washington, but to assemble all 787s in Washington, period.

This brought the outsourcing issue back to the forefront, and it shook the community's confidence all over again. This wasn't just about union workers. The entire state of Washington was now impacted. Strikes, job losses, successes – any of these things could cause a chain reaction throughout the community. Everybody was in the game.

We attempted to find common ground to keep the 787 line in Washington. I tried to reason with the company, saying they didn't need to do this. I said we had the workers and the resources to provide everything and anything that a greenfield facility could provide. In fact, nobody could deliver the quality we had honed and perfected for decades.

All I got in response was that the company was considering new greenfield sites.

Boeing issued an RFP to several states including South Carolina, Texas, and Utah, encouraging them to submit proposals on what they would be willing to do to get the 787 program. It became clear that Boeing had no intention to keep the second line in Washington, that a greenfield site was always the target. At the time South Carolina was the home of Boeing General Counsel Mike Luttig, who was influential in this move. This was all just a charade not only to the State of Washington but to all the other states that submitted RFPs.

The next time I heard from them was October 26, 2009, when Boeing announced that the second 787 line would be assembled in a new facility being built in Charleston, South Carolina. It would be a non-union facility filled with non-union workers.

This kicked sand in the face of everyone who built the first line.

Then came another media blitz aimed at discrediting the IAM and the engineers, informing the general public that the move from Puget Sound was all the union's fault. This, of course, was total bullshit.

About a week later, the new president of Boeing Commercial, Jim Albaugh, commented on the decision to build the plant in Charleston in an on-camera interview. "The overriding factor was not the business climate," he admitted. "And it was not the wages we're paying today. It was that we can not afford to have a work stoppage, you know, every three years. This will teach them a lesson."

Boom.

There it was, and we had it on tape.

He was saying that the company's South Carolina decision was fueled by the fact that union workers have the right to band together and stand up for themselves. Boeing wanted workers who would not – or, better yet, *could not* – strike. Their move was clearly anti-union. It was a threat. It was intimidation.

And it was illegal. Boeing was guilty of bargaining in bad faith.

In March 2010, we filed two charges with the NLRB, contending Boeing had violated federal labor laws. The first charge was that it had bargained in bad faith. We asserted that while we were negotiating with the company to keep the assembly line in Washington, it never had any intention of staying. The second charge was coercion and intimidation.

Now we had leverage.

The regional director of the NLRB interviewed me. If the charges I put forth could be supported by facts, those charges would turn into complaints issued by the federal government. Those complaints would then get litigated in a federal court.

I was able to support my charges with facts.

Then, the rock fight began. Insults and allegations flew back and forth. The company was seething and falsely claiming that we were intent on displacing the workers in South Carolina. The Obama administration took a lot of heat from media companies and members of Congress.

"How can you allow this to happen to a good company?"

"Why do you hate South Carolina?"

I got several hate calls myself. One congressman rang me just to say, "This is all your fault, Rich. It's all your fucking fault."

To keep pushing forward, I scheduled meetings with the governor, state elected officials in Olympia (Democrats and Republicans), and members of Congress to set them straight on the facts and the mistruths that were flying all over the airwaves. Talking face-to-face with Congress members resulted in growing support and interest in our cause. Senator Claire McCaskill requested a briefing on the facts before she walked into a hearing with Mike Luttig. In that meeting, she defended us against all the misinformation and harsh words.

The lawsuit did not move quickly through the NLRB. It stretched on for the rest of 2010 and then deep into 2011. Boeing sweated it the whole time. Gradually, it dawned on me what was happening. This was a very big deal, and the political pressure surrounding it was palpably intense. Everyone felt it. I realized that the NLRB was most likely going to drop one of the charges, simply to ease some of the tension.

We reviewed the possible outcomes with our attorneys. The penalty for bargaining in bad faith would be that the company would be forced to go back to the bargaining table with the union and negotiate until an agreement or an impasse was reached. The penalty for coercion and intimidation could be as severe as a legal order forcing them to stop building the South Carolina facility.

I figured that, most likely, the NLRB would drop the more severe complaint, which was coercion and intimidation. That would then put us back at the bargaining table, and I knew *that* would get us nowhere fast.

Quickly, we dropped the "bargaining in bad faith" charge.

Now, there was just the one. Coercion and intimidation.

The charge became an official federal complaint.

Boeing was outraged. It was a great moment.

The next step was the trial. We'd have our attorneys and the NLRB representing us. It was set to take place in Seattle Federal Court. This meant there would be depositions, testimony, and the potential embarrassment of Boeing executives. But it wasn't our goal to embarrass Boeing management. Our goal was to secure work for the employees.

The company was about to start planning a new plane, the 737 MAX. We decided to focus on that. It was now October 2011. The next contract negotiations were set for 2012.

We were in a good position. Just like back in 2008 when the company had to stop the hemorrhaging of money, it was now in a place where it had to stop the hemorrhaging of reputation. Boeing Company CEO Jim McNerney needed the lawsuit to go away. However reluctantly, the company was back at the table with us. They stayed noncommittal on the location where the MAX would be built. They had already put the 787 plant in Charleston, so finding a new city for the MAX was not out of the question. This threat of outsourcing was still their greatest leverage.

The NLRB suit loomed over our talks like a specter, and that was *our* leverage.

Senate Majority Leader Harry Reid, a friend of mine, took an interest in the issue. He called me to his office for a private meeting and asked me to brief him on the whole story. He had heard Boeing's side from senators and staff, and now he wanted to hear the union's side. I brought him up to date and told him we were entering negotiations.

"If we get a deal, I promise you'll be the first to know," I said.

As I was leaving the Capitol, one of Harry's staffers chased me down, caught me, and said, "Sorry, Rich, Harry wants to talk to you again."

I went back to his office and saw him looking at his schedule for the day. "Rich! You have to see this. Guess who I'm scheduled to meet with later today?" He showed me his calendar. He had a 5:30 meeting set with Jim McNerney. "Now I'm prepared," he said. "Our meeting was so timely. Thanks again for bringing me up to date."

Meanwhile, we went back to the table with Boeing. We negotiated. It was early, so contract talks were not on anyone's radar yet. We didn't publicize the talks, so only the bargaining committee knew they were going on. There were three of us from the union – former IAM District President Mark Blondin, District 751 President Tom Wroblewski, and me, the GVP. Boeing had two VPs at the table – Ray Conner and Rick Stephens. The talks went on for weeks, both in person and on the phone.

Soon we got the broad strokes figured out, so we began to focus on the details. These negotiations went smoothly and renewed relations between the union and the company. We arrived at a deal and granted Boeing its greatest wish – we withdrew the NLRB complaint. It was November 29, 2011.

I wanted to make good on my promise to Harry Reid. It was a Tuesday night, and I knew Harry met with the Democrat senators every Wednesday morning for a 7:30 breakfast. I called his home at 5:30 the next morning. His wife answered, then passed the phone to Harry.

I gave him the news. I asked him to announce it to his membership at the breakfast.

He was delighted and said he would, adding, "I'm gonna love doing this."

It was a good day. Harry announced the deal to Congress. We announced it to our members, and I followed up with a briefing for all state and federal officials. Boeing awarded us the MAX assembly and a comprehensive economic package that maintained thousands of jobs. It felt like the dawning of a new era.

There was peace for a little while, then Boeing announced its intention to build a new 777X in the U.S. The company started a bidding process that included several states, again making it clear that the Puget Sound did not have a lock on the next-generation airplane.

The first generation of the 777 included the transfer of wing technology and production to Mitsubishi in Japan. At the time, engineers in the aerospace industry thought the intentional transfer of wing tech to a foreign corporation was a big mistake. The new 777X would remedy this by keeping the new technology in the States. Boeing began a vetting process around the country, speaking to various governors and putting together a list of perspective non-Washington locations. While this was a real threat to the workers in the Puget Sound, at the same time, we knew we had a trump card – the knowledge and skill levels of our workers.

It felt crazy, but even as those negotiations were going on, something bigger was happening with me. It was July 2013. I was now 65.

It was time for me to retire. Time to step down as GVP.

My retirement party was one of those nights that goes by in the blink of an eye yet stays with you forever. Everyone showed up – senators, union leaders, company representatives, friends, family. I felt equal parts humble and proud as they celebrated this night with me. Was it really 45 years ago that I walked into GE as the newest welder on the floor? It certainly didn't feel like it.

We held the party in a major hotel on Capitol Hill, where all night my colleagues reflected on what we'd accomplished over the course of my tenure. We talked about our collaboration with companies. We talked about the legislators and the legislation. We remembered the more contentious issues that pulled me into the ring – the asbestos fight in the '80s, the NAFTA fight in the '90s, the constant attack on airline pensions in the '00s. I was continually reminded of achievements and losses, big and small. But as much as I reveled in the whole affair, one thought echoed around in the back of my mind all night:

*I'm not done.*

Yes, I was still embroiled in the 777X negotiations, and I would see those through before I left for good. But that's not what caused this feeling. I just wasn't ready to downshift yet. I wasn't tired. I wasn't bored. I certainly wasn't sick of the work. I was retiring simply because I was at retirement age, and those were our rules.

I accepted my fate, though it turned out I was far from finished.

As soon as I officially retired, IAM President Buffenbarger hired me on as a consultant to finish up the 777X negotiations. It engulfed my full attention for the rest of the year. I never predicted that these very talks would culminate in the largest, most comprehensive manufacturing labor contract in the history of labor contracts at the time.

Because I was deeply aware of the issues at play, Buffenbarger kept me involved in the Boeing talks. I was no longer GVP, but I was the top representative for "the International," a nickname for our union headquarters – *international* because we had members in Canada as well as the U.S.

At the negotiating table, I was, in essence, "the International." The term stood for what I represented, but in a way, it also became my title.

I was back in the fight.

As summer turned to autumn, the negotiations continued. What we did not know at the time was that Boeing was far enough along in the process to open in another state that they were already focusing on a few specific cities. These cities where tripping over themselves to boost the incentive packages to entice Boeing to move to their state.

Boeing's deciding factors were all based on money. They needed uninterrupted airplane production, and they needed it faster than humanly possible. Their backorder was enormous.

My deciding factors were all based on people. To me, these choices were about families, sustainable communities, and security for future generations of workers. Not only did we have tens of thousands of Boeing members in the Puget Sound region, but these union members had children who one day would need jobs. And then their children.

As the process went on, Boeing made it clear that they were simultaneously visiting state capitals to meet with the various governors and state legislators and hear their offers. The most aggressive states were Texas and Utah, as both had plenty of cash on hand to throw the company's way.

One of Boeing's sticking points in these negotiations was to stop the existing pension plan and transition to a savings plan. The fact of the matter was that Boeing's St. Louis facility, repped by the IAM, already agreed to this idea. In addition, Boeing's competitors, including IAM members at Lockheed, had made similar internal moves.

Boeing put together a proposal for the bargaining committee that included the elimination of the pension plan and its replacement with a 401(k), the building of a special new 1.5 million square foot facility for new wing technology, the 777X program remaining in the Puget Sound, and a cap on out-of-pocket health care costs. Also, they would extend the contract on the 737 MAX until 2024 with the promise of creating thousands of new jobs in the area.

The bargaining committee rejected the proposal. They were outraged.

It was the loss of the pension. Dismantling something that had been reliable for years and installing a new system was just a bridge too far. Boeing insisted they would not build the planes in Washington if they had to keep the pension plan. But taking away our member's pension made them feel disrespected by the company. Unvalued.

When Boeing learned the first proposal had been rejected, they accelerated their pursuit of non-union locations for the new plants. They had received proposals from 22 states, and they were considering over 50 potential sites. The bargaining committee and Boeing were under tremendous pressure from local politicians and community leaders to get an agreement.

About a month after the bargaining committee rejected the proposal, Boeing proposed a significantly modified proposal, though it still eliminated the pension plan. They made it clear this was their final offer and, if rejected, they would choose another site on which to manufacture the 777X and new wing facility.

Time was running out. I asked the bargaining committee to have the membership vote on this last and final offer – it was their future at stake, so let them decide. But most of the bargaining committee refused even to allow a vote. Some of them went so far as to say that the membership could not be trusted with a vote like this, implying they were not smart enough.

It was the committee's responsibility to represent all members in a fair manner, and this was a blatant breach of their duty. The members needed to know the facts – the company's proposal and intentions. They had the right to decide their fate. If they rejected it, fine. If they accepted it, fine. But a matter as large as this, that will affect 27,000 people and their families, *must* be voted on.

During this time the membership knew that Boeing was after the pension. They were showing up at local lodge meetings where District President Tom Wroblewski and Aerospace Coordinator Mark Johnson were answering questions about the company proposals. They were not trying to persuade the members, they were simply communicating facts so the members could vote informed.

As soon as Tom brought up the pension plan, though, the

members exploded into immediate outrage. They took it out on Tom. He explained to them that the offer brought job security and thousands of new positions. They didn't care. He explained that upon rejection of this deal, Boeing would react by choosing an alternative site for the MAX. They still didn't care.

At first, Tom remained cool under the pressure. But try as he might, he just could not convince the members that the company's threat was real. Then, he switched directions and swung over to their way of thinking. He tore his notes in half and announced that there would *not* be a vote after all.

He repeated this type of behavior at the other local lodge meetings he attended.

When Boeing got news of this, they announced to the press that we had rejected their best and final offer.

I had to work fast. I had to exhaust all options before the company officially announced a new facility in a new state. I needed our members to vote. It was my obligation and duty to ensure that every member had the opportunity to examine the proposal in detail, to ask questions, and to cast their vote by secret ballot for their future. This was not an "us against them" scenario. The company had leverage in the form of their threat to move facilities and jobs to another state. Was that right? No. Was it reality? Yes.

I worked with my team every day for a month, only taking a break on Christmas. I wanted to cover every angle and not leave anything to chance. There had to be a vote, regardless of the outcome.

I talked to Tom Wroblewski. I told him we *had* to have a vote.

He maintained that the price Boeing asked was too high. I urged him to let our members make that decision, to let them see the whole deal.

He wouldn't allow it.

I presented the facts to Buffenbarger, and he was very clear that the people needed to decide their fate. As president of the IAM he ordered the vote. We distributed materials that did not recommend acceptance or rejection, they just stated the facts.

The IAM secretary treasure office has responsibility for accuracy and auditing IAM records. Robert Roach, the Secretary Treasurer at the time, assigned his auditing staff to all locations that were conducting the votes to ensure that each member would be able to cast their ballots without fear of intimidation. We are a democratic union.

We set the vote for the first Friday of the new year.

It was the most harrowing vote of all, and the results were close – 51% voted to accept the proposal, 49% to reject it. By a very narrow margin, the members accepted the offer. The win for me was getting the vote to happen. Now that the members decided, we needed to move on and look at the positive side of the deal and how it was going to enhance their economic lives. To me this was a win for families in more ways than one.

First, there were our members' families in Washington. "If you're a young person," I told the press, "you've got a future here in aerospace. Parents and grandparents should be happy."

Then there was the IAM family. When the press asked me about local districts not agreeing with headquarters, I told them, "We're a family. Families have differences. There's nothing wrong with people having different opinions. We just have to grow together again." And I meant that. I knew there was an internal rift over this deal, but I also knew that the union could heal from it and become even stronger because of it. This deal that we just ratified benefited everyone eventually.

As it turns out, Boeing invested more than a billion and a half dollars into the State of Washington. The company built a new 1.5 million square-foot facility for wing construction and revamped its manufacturing operations.

It also hired 9,000 dues-paying members. It was the largest economic package to be negotiated by a manufacturing union in history.

Today the membership stands at 36,000. And the IAM Strike Fund was protected and has maintained its solvency for ten years.

We had fought well.

At last, I was ready to retire.

# AFTERWORD

Throughout all those years of negotiations, Boeing missed out on opportunity after opportunity to build lasting and long-term relationships with its workers, the union, and the local communities. Instead, the company created a board of directors where not one member comes from Puget Sound. Sticking to an adversarial stance when it came to workers' concerns became business as usual, and now, ten years later, the company is reaping what it sowed. As I write this in January 2025, Boeing is suffering financially, having regulatory problems, and recovering from a two-month machinists strike that ended just a few weeks ago. The company announced that that it now plans to cut 10% of its work force – 17,000 employees – due to an "overstaffing problem."

This and all the stories compiled here highlight the accumulation of anti-union sentiments and initiatives over time. Big business swayed politicians to give it the power to break unions. And it got it.

The U.S. Treasury reports that in the 1950s, 31% of U.S. workers were unionized. By 1977, it says, only 24% of U.S. workers were unionized. Today, that number stands at 13%. The Machinists Union itself has lost almost 150,000 members since 2002.

The two most significant and consequential events that led to the destruction of the American middle class were the passage of NAFTA and granting PNTR to China. Nonprofit consumer advocacy organization Public Citizen maintains that NAFTA cost U.S. 4.3 million jobs to date, and Coalition for a Prosperous America details how China's entrance into the WTO cost America 3.8 million jobs to date. Both of these disasters were executed under Democratic leadership in the country, and thus began the turn of the jaded no-longer middle class from blue to red.

Had we succeeded with the Striker Replacement Bill in the early 90s, unions and workers would have had leverage against the effects of NAFTA. Big business got everything it wanted, including destabilizing unions and withholding from workers any power in a strike. Communities by the thousands suffered. Millions of Americans fell bitterly and resentfully into poverty.

"To all the forgotten men and women who have been neglected, abandoned, and left behind, you will be forgotten no longer," promised a campaigning Donald Trump during the 2024 GOP National Convention.

The stage had been set when he ran in 2016; and to his good fortune, it had been set by Democrats. He saw that people were angry and frustrated beyond belief, so he shrewdly took advantage of that emotion. Instead of speaking in facts and concrete plans, he preached xenophobia and a vague revolution. He kept his rhetoric in appeals to emotion, so voters would stay whipped up into a frenzy.

He vociferously called NAFTA "the worst trade deal ever," and most Americans agreed with him. Like a gallant ship captain, he steered that emotion where he needed it, lofting the sails with promises of not only redemption, but revenge. Then, throughout his entire first term, he gave those millions of "forgotten" souls no practical solution. He had no remedy. All he did afford them was permission to hate louder.

And as we've mentioned above, he continued to use the same tactic through his 2024 campaign, and again it worked. It remains to be seen as of this writing how his second term will play out, but it's safe to say our 47th president will not do much to help organized labor.

Let's also acknowledge the positive here. President Joe Biden walked in solidarity with the UAW picket line in 2023. Also that year, Los Angeles saw a substantial series of effective union demonstrations. The service employees union (SEIU) went on strike, and the teachers union stood with them in solidarity. This resulted in a happy resolution of the SEIU's demands *and* leverage for the teachers to use in their own contract negotiations. Also, both the writers guild and actors union went on long strikes until their demands were heard and addressed by the studios. As Kamala Harris ran for president in 2024, she praised the value of unions and the importance of a renewed manufacturing base in the United States. People are waking up to the situation. There are those in the younger generations who are noticing that when people bond together, they form a power greater than the sum of its parts. They are beginning to value the benefit of collective bargaining. But that alone will not bring unions back.

We still have a long way to go if we ever want to build up to that same level of strength and confidence workers enjoyed in 1950s, 60s, and 70s. Members of Congress have successfully stalled and weakened labor protections for the past forty years. Today's laws favor anti-union employers, and the dissolution of pension plans and disappearance of benefits has become normalized. It's been like this for so long that it's going to take time and a radical change to save the American worker. People need to acknowledge the destructive greed inherent in our business laws and loudly assert that enough is enough!

There is always hope. New leaders will emerge – leaders who believe in the future, who won't tolerate excuses by politicians, who are ready to make a difference and reverse this downward spiral. But the only way that will happen is if we continue this dialogue and give proper attention to those hundreds of suffering and struggling communities in our country that feel they've been forgotten and left to die.

As unions go, so does the rest of the workforce. The strength of unions is always a bellwether of the health and happiness of the American worker. Let's meet our potential for greatness. Let's remember it's not just our future at stake here – it's our children's future, and their children's future. That's why now more than ever it is essential we stay in the fight!

R.M.
January 25, 2025

www.ingramcontent.com/pod-product-compliance
Lightning Source LLC
Chambersburg PA
CBHW051307120626
46547CB00015B/2132